Successful
Living
Skills

Successful Living Skills

The Puzzle of Families

Leni Cowling
M.Ed., LPC, HRD

Bellaire, Michigan

Published by Family-Information
PO Box 892
Bellaire, MI 49615

Publisher's Cataloging-in-Publication Data
Cowling, Leni.
      Successful living skills: the puzzle of families / Leni Cowling—Bellaire, MI:
Family-Information, 2002.
          p   ;   cm.

      ISBN 0-9715106-0-1
      1. Family 2. Parenting 3. Parenthood 4. Interpersonal relations I. Title

HQ734.C69   2002   2002091496
306.87   -dc21   CIP

06 05 04 03 02 • 5 4 3 2 1

Cover and book design by Barbara Hodge
Project coordination by Jenkins Group • www.bookpublishing.com

Printed in the United States

Table of Contents

Self-Esteem

I Want to Believe in Myself

SECTION

1

Self-Esteem

 When you talk to yourself, you are listening. What do you say to yourself? How do you speak? Are you critical? Are you judgmental? Are you negative? Or, are you understanding, positive and reasonable? When you communicate with others, you use the same kind of talk that you use on yourself. To have positive relationships, we must nurture and support our friends, and the first friend we make is with our own self. How do we come to value our own self?

Self-Esteem is the price tag we wear for ourselves. It is made up of self-respect and self-worth. Self-respect is when we can trust ourselves to know and do the right thing. Self-worth is when we can count on ourselves to be able to take care of ourselves adequately.

The six building blocks of self -esteem that you need are:

1) **Sense of physical safety:**
   In the home
   In the school
   In the neighborhood

2) **Sense of emotional security**
   A right to feel happiness, sadness, fear and joy.

3) **Sense of identity**
   As childhood unfolds in the various stages of development, the self-hood is never ridiculed or denied and has a sense of dignity.

4) **Sense of belonging**
   You belong to an individual or group of individuals, the family, who claim and value you.

5) **Sense of competency**
   You learn to take care of yourself and   learn the ability to care for others and things.

6) **Sense of purpose**
   You have a personhood and a place that the rest of us would miss, should you not be around. The world is a better place because you live!

Good parenting provides a framework for building self-esteem.

How You can Hypnotize Yourself into Failure

Your behavior is largely determined by the words you use. You think in words. You plan out your life by words. You talk to yourself in words. You have spent all your life hypnotizing yourself. Every word you repeat and believe tends to shape what you become.

Take a look at the words you might use that have a negative effect on your life. These words are negative affirmations. They are negative needs that take root and grow.

1. "I can't quit smoking!"
2. "I can't remember people's names!"
3. "I'll never be a wealthy person!"
4. "I'm not perfect!"
5. "I don't have much patience!"
6. "I have a poor memory!"
7. "I don't have as much zip as I used to!"
8. "I just can't get along with him/her!"
9. "I hate food that I have never tasted!"
10. "I'm not as smart as other people!"
11. "I can't lose weight because I can't stick to a diet!"
12. "I just can't seem to get going in the morning!"
13. "I don't like my job!"
14. "I've got too much work to do!"
15. "I just haven't felt too good lately!"
16. "I need a vacation!"
17. "I get nervous around strangers!"
18. "I never had a chance!"
19. "I'm too old to change!"
20. "I don't have any special talent!"
21. "I can't think of things to talk about to people!"
22. "I think that the children get on my nerves all the time!"
23. "I just can't seem to save any money!"
24. "I'm very self-conscious!"
25. "I just can't help it! I worry a lot!"
26. "I'm so stupid!"
27. "I'm not very good looking!"
28. "I can't do anything about this!"
29. "I'm not able to learn to do new things!"
30. "I can't control my anger!"

Can you think of ways that you have hypnotized yourself? What happened as a result? What do you think you need to do in the future? Write it down.

Basic Assertive Rights

I have the right to ...

1) judge my own behavior, thoughts and emotions and to take the responsibility for their initiation and consequences upon myself. I have the right to be the ultimate judge of myself.

2) be treated with respect, to be listened to and taken seriously, not patronized.

3) feel proud about what's good about myself.

4) refuse requests without having to feel guilty or selfish.

5) feel and express anger.

6) feel and express a healthy competitiveness and achievement drive.

7) strive for self-actualization through whatever ethical channels my talents and interests find natural.

8) use my judgment in deciding which needs are the most important for me to meet.

9) have my opinions given the same respect and consideration that other people's opinions are given.

10) be treated as a capable human adult and not to be patronized.

11) have my needs be as important as the needs of other people.

12) be independent.

13) offer no reasons or excuses to justify my behavior.

14) judge whether I am responsible for finding solutions to other people's problems.

15) change my mind.

16) make mistakes and be responsible for them.

17) say, "I don't know!"

18) being independent of the goodwill of others.

19) be illogical in making decisions.

20) say, "I don't understand!"

21) say, "I don't care!"

What area in your life needs to be strengthened with your rights?
What can you say and do to accomplish that?

Make a list of people who you admire. What do you like about them?

_____

_____

_____

_____

_____

_____

Make a list of people you do not like. What don't you like about them?

_____

_____

_____

_____

_____

What do you like about yourself?

I like me because

_____

_____

_____

_____

_____

_____

My Family Tree

You have a genetic linkage to all of your ancestors. How far back can you go? Knowing this history can help you make a difference in your own life. For example, diabetes or heart conditions in your family can be prevented with the right health attitudes. You and your children can benefit. **Include brothers and sisters.**

(Name, Date of Birth, and Date of Death)

My Great-Grandparents:

_____

_____

My Grandparents:

_____

_____

My Parents:

_____

_____

Me: (and my brothers and sisters)

_____

_____

_____

My Children:

_____

_____

_____

The father of my children:

_____

Our Family's History

Our family came from _____

They lived in _____

They earned a living as _____

The reason they came to America was _____

The first in the family to come to America were _____

The year they came was approximately _____

They traveled by _____

Family members they left behind _____

The first to arrive in America settled in _____

Their home was in _____

They earned a living by _____

Stories about their early life in America as told by _____

Memorable historic events in their lifetime were _____

People who influenced their generation were _____

Inventions and discoveries in their lifetime _____

How society changed during their lifetime _____

Ways life was harder then _____

Ways the world was better then _____

Maternal Grandmother and Grandfather

Grandmother's name _____

date of birth/death _____

Name we called her _____

She was born in _____

She grew up in _____

Her faith _____

Her education _____

Grandma worked as _____

She loved to _____

Special talents and creativity she had _____

They were married on _____

Hardships they faced were _____

My favorite memories of them _____

Grandfather's name _____

date of birth/death _____

Name we called him _____

He was born in _____

He grew up in _____

His faith _____

His education _____

Grandfather worked as _____

He loved to _____

Special talents and creativity he had _____

They had _____ children named _____

They enjoyed doing these things together _____

Favorite family stories _____

Maternal Grandmother and Grandfather *(same information as above)*

How far back in your family's history can you go?

When you look at your family and family history, you may find many of the beliefs you hold. These beliefs can be good and they can also be bad. If you can honestly examine them, you may find ways to overcome the bad beliefs and go on to make your own life more successful.

Developing Self-Confidence

1. How does your concern over what someone else might think of you affect your self-confidence?

2. How does the fear of failure affect people's lives? How about your life?

3. In what way do you compare yourself with others? How does it affect your self-confidence?

4. In what ways do you counteract or even sabotage yourself?

5. In what situations do you have self-confidence? What are some of the ways you lack self-confidence?

6. How are the two different?

7. It is said that we think of ourselves in negative terms. How do you feel about this? How would it apply to you?

8. If you "act" more self-confident, can you "feel" more self-confident? In what ways can you act more self-confident?

My Self-Image

When you "see" yourself in your mind, what is the mental image you have?
What image do you think other people have of you?

1. To work on self-esteem, get to know yourself and others as unique and one-of-a-kind individual's that you are. Try to become more in tune with other people by attempting to see, hear and feel what they have experienced. Be honest about yourself and your feelings with other people. Accept yourself. When you know and like who you are, you will be more able to become the person you would like to be.

2. Are you working on your health by not smoking, maintaining good nutrition, a healthy weight and eating something fresh and unprocessed every day; getting adequate fiber, water and calcium; controlling alcohol, cholesterol and caffeine intake?

3. Are you scheduling and keeping regular appointments for physical, visual, dental, emotional and all other men's/women's health needs?

4. Are you continually evaluating your physical appearance, and changing when appropriate, to meet your specific age needs in hair length and style, clothing length and style, shoes, etc?

5. Are you keeping an active, but varied and balanced schedule, which includes leisure time for yourself to play or reward yourself?

6. Are you surrounding yourself with supportive and optimistic friends who possess a healthy sense of humor?

7. Are you sharing yourself by contributing to at least one meaningful cause, in government, church/synagogue, community, special projects, etc.?

8. Are you challenging yourself to develop or learn new skills, languages, hobbies, sports, interests and/or activities?

Sometimes we can feel overwhelmed and unable to cope.

Which do you imagine yourself doing when you need to cope?

Assert myself   Contact one of my supports

Change a habit   Help someone

Go shopping   Listen to my favorite music

Eat something healthy   Exercise

Take a trip   Take a break

Learn something new   Go to a movie

Write in a journal   Read a book or magazine

Take a walk   Talk to a friend

Take a hot bath or shower   Take a nap

Recognizing the importance of these valuable tools is the first step in establishing coping skills. The next step is exercising these skills when feeling depressed, to increase your sense of well-being!

What do you wish for? If you could have anything you want, what would you wish for? Write it here:

_____

_____

_____

_____

What do you see yourself doing in five years? Write it here:

_____

_____

_____

_____

How do you see your wishes being fulfilled? Write it here:

_____

_____

_____

_____

Choices

You have probably heard the saying, "We learn with experience and experience comes from making bad choices!" Do you agree with this statement? Have you ever regretted a bad choice? What did you learn from it? Was it especially painful? Could you have found a way to make a better choice?

For example, choose one:

1. Which season do you like best?
   ___ Winter
   ___ Summer
   ___ Fall
   ___ Spring

2. Which do you think is the most harmful?
   ___ cigarettes
   ___ marijuana
   ___ overeating
   ___ alcohol

3. Which would you least like to be?
   ___ Disfigured
   ___ Very sickly
   ___ Blind
   ___ Deaf

4. Where would you rather live?
   ___ on a farm
   ___ in the suburbs
   ___ in an inner city
   ___ in another country

5. Which would you like to do most?
   ___ Travel by automobile
   ___ Travel by bus
   ___ Travel by airplane
   ___ Travel by train

6. Which would you least like to be?
   ___ a prison guard
   ___ a garbage collector
   ___ a meat butcher
   ___ a funeral director

7. In which of these situations would you be most likely to take some action?
   ___ A car is parked with its headlights on in broad daylight.
   ___ A scared a kitten is high in a tree.
   ___ A child is crying alone in the street.

8. If you were with your family in a boat that capsized far from shore and there was only one life preserver, would you
   ___ save your mate
   ___ save one of your children
   ___ save yourself

See? You do make choices every minute of every day and some of these choices require a bit of thought. It helps to discuss the choices with someone else to get their opinion. However, the choice you make is yours alone and you do not have to make the same choice as everyone else.

 **Priorities**

What is important to you in your personal relations and life experiences? Rate these items on a scale of one to ten. (Ten being the highest value and one being the lowest.) Then share your results with someone else and discuss why you decided to make that choice. Choose a number only once.

_____ A close-knit family

_____ A loving relationship

_____ Physical attractiveness

_____ A satisfying marriage

_____ Two months of vacation a year

_____ A chance to be creative

_____ The freedom to make your own decisions

_____ Make a difference in the world

_____ A beautiful home

_____ Perfect health

_____ Unlimited travel

_____ Honesty with friends

_____ A sensuous sex life

_____ A large, personal library

_____ Peace in the world

_____ Being treated fairly

_____ Confidence in yourself

_____ Influence and power in your community

_____ A high spiritual experience

_____ A secure religious faith

_____ Dependable transportation

_____ Someone who needs you

_____ Someone to take care of you

_____ Orderly personal affairs

_____ Great wealth

_____ Quitting drugs or alcohol

_____ Losing weight

_____ Becoming famous

Problem Solving

So many people are fearful of making decisions, so they avoid making them. In fact, people are taught to exist with problems rather than making decisions and doing something about them. For those who think that there is only one solution to a problem, they are mistaken. Actually, there can be several perfectly workable solutions for any problem. So, any one may be tried and changed if found inadequate.

To handle problems, you need to determine what the real problem is first. What are the things that contribute to the problem? Is there more than one problem involved? To whom is it a problem? Who is involved? What is involved?

Next, think about what you expect to achieve by handling the problem? If it could be solved, what would the results be? If you take action, what objectives do you have in mind?

Then, gather facts about the problem. Get other's opinions. When you have gotten enough information to feel you can take action on it, you then need to think about as many solutions, answers, or actions for the problem as you can. Here, you can be very creative. Sometimes, creativity can be fun to solve problems.

Now, it is time to choose a course of action to follow. If you make a wrong choice, you can go back and choose another course of action.

The best part is that you will be making choices, solving problems and finding your own independence in the process. This will give you self-confidence and more self-esteem. You can accomplish all you wish to achieve!

Tackling problems—one at a time

What do you feel is the biggest problem that you are facing right now?

_____

_____

_____

_____

_____

Can you think of some future difficulties that could develop if you do not do something about this problem now?

_____

_____

_____

_____

_____

_____

And if you do nothing?

_____

_____

_____

_____

_____

If you have chosen to do something about your biggest problem now, what are some of the choices you have? List them here.

1. _____

_____

_____

2. _____

_____

_____

3. _____

_____

_____

Now list some pros and cons of those possible choices.

PRO	CON
_____	_____
_____	_____
_____	_____
_____	_____
_____	_____

Can you see the advantage of one particular choice over another?

_____

_____

_____

_____

What will you choose to do?

_____

_____

What do you feel is the second biggest problem that you are facing right now?

_____

_____

_____

_____

_____

Can you think of some future difficulties that could develop if you do not do something about this problem?

_____

_____

_____

_____

_____

_____

And if you do nothing?

_____

_____

_____

_____

_____

If you have chosen to do something about your second biggest problem now, what are some of the choices you have? List them here.

1. _____

_____

_____

2. _____

_____

_____

3. _____

_____

_____

Now list some pros and cons of those possible choices.

PRO	CON
_____	_____
_____	_____
_____	_____
_____	_____
_____	_____

Can you see the advantage of one particular choice over another?

_____

_____

_____

_____

What will you choose to do?

_____

_____

The Rules of Being Human

Make Your Dreams Come True!

1. When you were conceived, you received a body. You may like it or hate it,
   but it will belong to you for the entire period of this lifetime.

2. During this lifetime, you will learn lessons. You are enrolled in a full-time
   informal school called life. Each day in this school you will have the
   opportunity to learn lessons. You may like the lessons or think them stupid or irrelevant. These lessons are yours.

3. There are no mistakes, only lessons. Growth is a process of trial and
   error, with experimentation. The "failed" experiments that have caused
   pain and disappointment are as much a part of the process as the experiments that are "successful" and have given you happiness.

4. The lessons are important and are repeated until they are learned. A lesson can be presented to you in various forms until you have learned it. Then, you can go on to the next lesson.

5. Your educational lessons do not end. There is no part of life that does not contain its own lessons. If you are alive, there are lessons to be learned and you will continue to have lessons until the end of life. When you decide to consider them "interesting" and worthy of your attention, you will make great progress.

6. "The grass looks greener on the other side" is often heard, but in reality, if you get in the other side, the same is true.

7. You can see yourself by the reaction that others make to you. They are merely mirrors of you. You cannot love or hate something about another person unless it reflects to you something you love or hate about yourself.

8. What you make of your life is up to you. You have all the tools and resources you need and what you choose to do with them is up to you. You have many choices.

9. All the answers lie inside of you. You need to go to a quiet place and be alone and talk to yourself with honesty and feelings. If you are a person you can trust, you will find the company is good, then you will recognize others who can be trusted also and bring them into your life. Your life is of great importance to you. Your life is also of great importance to others.

Time Management

SECTION
2

Time Management

Time management is very much the process of getting organized so you have the time and space to do what you want to do, having fun and enjoying the day. The following list is all aspects of this organization.

- **Home Evaluation Survey—making an assessment of the home and the needed repairs or maintenance schedule.** (See chapter on Home Management for checklist.)

- **Money Management System**—putting a system together so money coming in and going out is not wasted and the bills are paid on time. (See chapter on Money Management for checklist.)

- **Home Organizer**—Chore sheets for a schedule of cleaning and maintaining a clean and organized home in the kitchen. (See chapter on Home Management for checklists.)

> Bathroom—(bathing area, linen closet, makeup area, toilet, dressing area)
>
> Bedrooms—(sleeping area, dressing area, closet area)
>
> Living rooms—(TV area, reading area, talking area, video/CD storage)
>
> Kitchen—(prepare food area, dining area, pantry, recipe area)
>
> Office/library—(computer area, desk area, bookshelves, file cabinets)
>
> Craft room—(craft storage, sewing area, painting area)
>
> Workshop—(tool storage, workbench, storage space)
>
> Garden—(tool storage, storage for mower, tiller, etc., potting area)

- **Meal Planner**—a plan for the meals for a month, using a shopping list, a weekly meal planning chart and the organization of staple items so you don't "run out" or buy double because you forgot you already had some. (See chapter on Food and Nutrition for checklists.)

- **Moving Planner**—a timely schedule for packing and moving to reduce the stress and loss of things. (See chapter of How to Find a Place to Live for checklists.)

- **Personal Organizer**—the use of a day timer, a place where important papers are kept and family records. Also a place where goals can be written and progress managed.

Time for family exercise. If you or your family members are overweight, it will cost you in health and medical expenses and can be dangerous. This may need to be a priority in time until you get back into a healthy lifestyle. Every family member should have at least 30 minutes of active fitness a day, and when done as a family can be a lot of fun. Get out and breathe some fresh air!

How do you spend your time now? Color in the circle to see.

My 24-hour Day

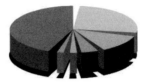

Each space is
1 hour of time

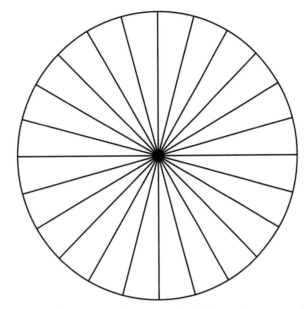

Do a typical weekday. Can you see where your time is going? Everything you do falls into four categories:

1. Those things that are important and urgent.
2. Those things that are important but not urgent.
3. Those things that are urgent, but not important.
4. Those things that are neither important nor urgent.

Can you sort out the things that you do every day into the four categories?
You need to decide which are the most important things to do, prioritize them, and then forget the rest until you can get around to it.

Making plans:

1. Prepare a daily list of things to do.
2. Mark the most important things.
3. Make a weekly plan.
4. Compare the weekly plan with the daily plan and re-prioritize your important things as needed.

For example: If you need to do the washing, as nobody has any clean clothes, and you need to pay the bills, which is most important to be done? You must choose. There are options too. Can you sit and pay the bills while you wait for the laundry? How will you get organized so that you can do this?

If you find yourself always in a crisis, you need to find out why this happens. What are the time wasters? Are you interrupted a lot? Are there telephone calls that make you stop what you are doing? Do you have unplanned visitors? How do you handle these?

What would you do if you had dinner ready on the table for your family and another family of six just dropped in? How would you handle this situation?

Do you put off doing things because you don't like them – such as budgeting? What happens when you put it off too long? What can you do to make the job a little pleasanter and easier? Taking small bites out of a large job can help, such as cleaning the basement. Rewarding yourself for steps taken can make it nicer too. Creating a pleasant place to do the task is helpful, if you can, or listening to music while you do it, if it does not distract you from the task. What can you do to help yourself? The way you deal with your time can teach your children important skills also.

Emergency Phone Numbers

Post the emergency phone numbers where they are close to each phone and can be easily seen in case of an emergency.

Fire Department _____   Police Department _____

Ambulance _____   Hospital _____

Poison Control _____   Pharmacy _____

Animal Control _____

Neighbors _____   Neighbors _____

My Dreams

If I could have whatever I wanted, what would my first wish be? _____
_____
_____
_____

How much money would I like to have? _____
_____
_____
_____

I would like to look like: _____
_____
_____
_____

I would like to have a job that: _____
_____
_____
_____

I would like to travel to: _____
_____
_____
_____

I would like to have friends that: _____
_____
_____
_____

I would like a partner that: _____
_____
_____
_____

My Goals

My life goal is to: _____
_____
_____
_____
_____

In three years, I would like to: _____
_____
_____
_____
_____

In five years, I would like to: _____
_____
_____
_____
_____

In ten years, I would like to:_____
_____
_____
_____
_____

In twenty years, I would like to: _____
_____
_____
_____
_____

How will I get there?

My Three-Month Goals

Name: _____

Date: _____

Goal: Date Achieved: Comments:

- _____   _____   _____
- _____   _____   _____
- _____   _____   _____
- _____   _____   _____
- _____   _____   _____
- _____   _____   _____
- _____   _____   _____
- _____   _____   _____

My Six-Month Goals

Goal: Date Achieved: Comments:

- _____   _____   _____
- _____   _____   _____
- _____   _____   _____
- _____   _____   _____
- _____   _____   _____
- _____   _____   _____
- _____   _____   _____
- _____   _____   _____

Schedule of Projects

Project: _____

Estim. Completion Date: _____   Actual Completion Date: _____

Project: _____

Estim. Completion Date: _____   Actual Completion Date: _____

Project: _____

Estim. Completion Date: _____   Actual Completion Date: _____

Project: _____

Estim. Completion Date: _____   Actual Completion Date: _____

Project: _____

Estim. Completion Date: _____   Actual Completion Date: _____

Project: _____

Estim. Completion Date: _____   Actual Completion Date: _____

Project: _____

Estim. Completion Date: _____   Actual Completion Date: _____

Project: _____

Estim. Completion Date: _____   Actual Completion Date: _____

Project: _____

Estim. Completion Date: _____   Actual Completion Date: _____

Project: _____

Estim. Completion Date: _____   Actual Completion Date: _____

Project: _____

Estim. Completion Date: _____   Actual Completion Date: _____

Projects To Do

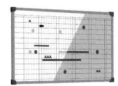

Type of Project _____

Start Date: _____ Target Date: _____ Completed: _____

Steps Taken to Date : _____

_____

Future Steps Needed: _____

Comments/Suggestions: _____

_____

Type of Project _____

Start Date: _____ Target Date: _____ Completed: _____

Steps Taken to Date : _____

_____

Future Steps Needed: _____

Comments/Suggestions: _____

_____

Type of Project _____

Start Date: _____ Target Date: _____ Completed: _____

Steps Taken to Date : _____

_____

Future Steps Needed: _____

Comments/Suggestions: _____

_____

Type of Project _____

Start Date: _____ Target Date: _____ Completed: _____

Steps Taken to Date : _____

_____

Future Steps Needed: _____

Comments/Suggestions: _____

_____

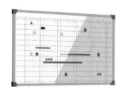

Project Update

Name: _____

Type of Project _____

Start Date: _____ Target Date: _____ Completed: _____

Steps Taken to Date : _____

_____

Future Steps Needed: _____

Comments/Suggestions: _____

_____

Type of Project _____

Start Date: _____ Target Date: _____ Completed: _____

Steps Taken to Date : _____

_____

Future Steps Needed: _____

Comments/Suggestions: _____

_____

Type of Project _____

Start Date: _____ Target Date: _____ Completed: _____

Steps Taken to Date : _____

_____

Future Steps Needed: _____

Comments/Suggestions: _____

_____

Type of Project _____

Start Date: _____ Target Date: _____ Completed: _____

Steps Taken to Date : _____

_____

Future Steps Needed: _____

Comments/Suggestions: _____

_____

Schedule for the year

Note important dates or activities that occur in each month of the year.

September	October
November	December
January	February
March	April
May	June
July	August

What needs to be done this month?

1st week:

2nd week:

3rd week:

4th week:

What needs to be done this week?

Monday:

Tuesday:

Wednesday:

Thursday:

Friday:

Saturday:

Sunday:

What needs to be done today?

6:00 _____	3:30 _____
6:30 _____	4:00 _____
7:00 _____	4:30 _____
7:30 _____	5:00 _____
8:00 _____	5:30 _____
8:30 _____	6:00 _____
9:00 _____	6:30 _____
9:30 _____	7:00 _____
10:00 _____	7:30 _____
10:30 _____	8:00 _____
11:00 _____	8:30 _____
11:30 _____	9:00 _____
Noon _____	9:30 _____
12:30 _____	10:00 _____
1:00 _____	10:30 _____
1:30 _____	11:00 _____
2:00 _____	11:30 _____
2:30 _____	Midnight_____
3:00 _____	

What needs to be done this week?

Monday:

Tuesday:

Wednesday:

Thursday:

Friday:

Saturday:

Sunday:

What needs to be done today?

6:00 _____

6:30 _____

7:00 _____

7:30 _____

8:00 _____

8:30 _____

9:00 _____

9:30 _____

10:00 _____

10:30 _____

11:00 _____

11:30 _____

Noon _____

12:30 _____

1:00 _____

1:30 _____

2:00 _____

2:30 _____

3:00 _____

3:30 _____

4:00 _____

4:30 _____

5:00 _____

5:30 _____

6:00 _____

6:30 _____

7:00 _____

7:30 _____

8:00 _____

8:30 _____

9:00 _____

9:30 _____

10:00 _____

10:30 _____

11:00 _____

11:30 _____

Midnight_____

Time Organization

Develop an overall strategy and define your priorities by:

Stop procrastinating. Start right now. Decide what you are going to do with the next piece of clutter that you pick up.

Everything you have will need to be cleaned, repaired and cared for—if you keep it. The less stuff you have, the less you have to spend on it. Keep those things you use regularly, or have value to you, and get rid of the everything else.

1. Dig out. Schedule a time for a specific clean-out job and don't let anything interfere with it. Closets, cupboards, pantry, garage, bedroom...organize one at a time.

2. Put on some lively music. Sing or dance along. It'll make you move faster and keep your spirits up.

3. Bring boxes. The first part of cleaning up is sorting things. Put similar things together. Arrange four or five boxes within easy reach. Then put things where they really belong. One box is for stuff to keep. The second box is for stuff to throw out. The third box is for stuff to give away. The fourth box is for stuff you are not sure where to put it. Keep the fourth box for three months. If you have not used anything in it during this time, it can be given away or thrown out. Perhaps you will want to make one box for a yard sale or consignment shop and another for a charity that takes discards.

4. Keep it out. It is too easy to get more "stuff" in. Make an inventory rule: If something new comes in, something old goes out. Once you are organized, you make a place for everything and keep everything in its place. Keep items as close as possible to their point of use. Don't buy anything unless you have someplace to keep it. Spend a few minutes each day picking up or discarding clutter and it won't overwhelm you again. Open mail and sort it as soon as you get it, putting papers into four boxes: to do, to pay, to file and to read. Throw the rest out. Write any appointments or invitations immediately on the calendar. Don't use the garage or basement as a dumping ground. A good de-junking every six months will keep you in control of your space, your time and your sanity. When you teach your children to be organized, they will have a life skill of great value that will last a lifetime.

Money Management

SECTION
3

Money Matters

When you get organized, it is much easier to keep track of your money in and outl.

1. Get a box for important papers.
In this box, label folders for each item of important information that you need to keep.

Educational Information
Your résumé
Your diplomas and certificates
Your educational and work experience information

Legal Certificates
Birth certificates, yours and your children's
Your marriage certificate
Death certificates
Divorce certificates
Any custody information and papers
Your will, Powers of Attorney, and legal documents

Insurance papers
Car insurance papers
House insurance papers
Renter's insurance papers
Health insurance papers
Business insurance papers
Life insurance papers

Credit cards
Credit card information and numbers
Credit check information
Land contracts or loan papers

Real Estate
Copies of real estate taxes
Deeds
Information on real estate

Investments
Stocks
Bonds
Bank accounts
Credit union accounts

Retirement
Pension information
Death and funeral planning papers
Executor papers

Money Management System

You need a daily system for organizing your bills and income.

2. Obtain a 3 inch loose-leaf binder and 13 large envelopes. Punch holes in the large envelopes to fit in the binder.

There are two ways to organize this information and you can choose which one you would prefer to use.

a. Label each large envelope with one month of the year (12), and one labeled "Taxes" for the whole year on the 13th envelope, which will provide the information for taxes. Place the envelopes in the binder.

Place **each** pay stub, the receipts from the grocery store and for any purchase you make, into the envelope for the month. This way, you will be able to go back into the month to see how much you spent on groceries, clothes, gas, electricity, telephone, and everything else.

At the end of the year, you must go back into the first envelope and take every thing out and start to sort into piles the various bills and pay stubs. Then, take the second envelope and sort it onto the piles too. Go through all 12 envelopes in the same manner, sorting out the various bills into their respective piles. After all the 12 envelopes have been emptied of their contents, place all of the piles into the 13th envelope and label this envelope for the year. Now you have all the information on your income and bills for the entire year. You must keep this information for seven years in case you need to go back. Find a box to store your tax envelopes in. After you have set up this system, you can throw out the envelopes that are over seven years old, and keep adding the present year envelopes.

b. The second way that you could choose to organize your money management system is to label the envelopes according to the subject, such as gas, electric, water, mortgage or rent, clothes, groceries, health – doctor and dentist bills, insurance, entertainment, income, investments, taxes. You may need to add additional envelopes for other subjects you need. However, at the end of the year, all the contents of the envelopes can be placed into an envelope and labeled with the year. This way, you will have all the information on your money management for the entire year. You must keep this information for seven years.

Labels for My Money Management Envelopes

Cut each month label and paste it on the edge of the 12 envelopes in your binder. Place the last label on the 13th envelope to file for taxes for the year. Put the label for Unpaid Bills on a box where you can see it easily and put all unpaid bills there until you pay them. Then put the receipts in your monthly folder.

JANUARY

FEBRUARY

MARCH

APRIL

MAY

JUNE

JULY

AUGUST

SEPTEMBER

OCTOBER

NOVEMBER

DECEMBER

TAXES FOR YEAR _____

UNPAID BILLS

Budgeting

Categorizing your money:

Taxes
Social Security
Federal
State and local

The roof over your head
Rent
Mortgage
Property taxes
Gas/electric/oil
Water/garbage
Phone
Cable TV
Furniture/appliances
Maintenance/repair

The food you eat
Groceries
Restaurants and takeout

Getting around
Car loan
Gasoline
Maintenance/repairs
State registration fees
Tolls and parking
Buses or subway fares

The clothes you wear
Clothing
Shoes
Jewelry/watches
Dry cleaning

Fun stuff you do
Entertainment/movies/concerts
Vacation and travel
Gifts
Hobbies
Pets

Looking Nice
Haircuts
Health club or gym
Makeup
Other

Educational Expenses
Course tuition
Books
Supplies
Lab/locker fees

Your health
Doctor
Prescription drugs
Dentist
Vision/glasses
Therapy

Insurance you need
Homeowners/renters
Auto
Health
Life
Disability

Children's care
Child support
Toys
Daycare expenses
School expenses/lunches

Repayment of debt
Credit/charge card
Auto loans
Student loans
Personal loans

Personal business
Accountant fees
Attorney fees
Financial advisor fees

Financial Guide

Spending Ranges

No two families spend money in exactly the same way but there are established ranges for different budget categories to use as a guide. If you exceed the range for an item or two, you must take it out of something else.

Category	Percent of Take-home pay
Housing	25 to 32%
Food (at home or out)	18 to 23%
Installment loans (including car payments)	10 to 20%
Transportation	7 to 12%
Savings	7 to 10%
Clothing	3 to 10%
Medical care	3 to 10%
Leisure activities	2 to 7%
Miscellaneous	3 to 5%

Assets:
(What you own)
Cash
Checking accounts
Savings and money market accounts
Certificates of deposit
Tax refunds due
Other money owed to you
Value of all securities:
    Stocks
    Bonds
    Mutual funds
Cash value of life insurance
Market value of home
Value of other real estate
Current value of cars
Other vehicles (boat, motorcycle, plane)
Value of home furnishings
Estimated worth of silver, furs, jewelry, etc.
Equity in your business
Vested interest in company pension or
    profit-sharing plan
Value of IRA, Keogh or 401-k plans
Value of annuities
Other assets
Total Assets

Liabilities:
(What you Owe)
Balance due on home mortgage
Other real estate loans
Auto loans
Education loans
Installment loans (furniture, appliances)
Other loans
Credit card balances
Charge accounts
Unpaid medical bills
Other unpaid bills
Taxes due
Other liabilities
Total Liabilities

Total Assets   _____

Minus – Total Liabilities   _____

Equals = Net Worth   _____

Can You Buy Happiness?

When you try to "buy Happiness," it is a temporary fix and often leads to guilt, depression, embarrassment, stress and even financial debt.

Do you:

1. Binge-buy? (clothes, shoes, "items on sale," groceries)
    The last time was _____

2. Buy status objects? (jewelry, cars, furniture, name-brand items)
    The last time was _____

3. Gamble excessively? (horse races, lottery tickets, card games, bingo)
    The last time was _____

4. Buy impulsively? (clothing, gadgets, fad items, CDs)
    The last time was _____

5. Spend excessively on others? (too expensive or too many gifts, excessively on charities)
    The last time was _____

6. Spend to avoid unpleasant situations (vacation, traveling to get away from problems)
    The last time was _____

Why do you do it? _____

If you wish, make a little card to carry in your wallet like this:

Am I Buying Happiness?????

Will I be happy with my purchase tomorrow… next week… next month?

Am I able to afford this?

Do I want to spend my money on this right now?

Why am I really buying this?

Am I OK with my reason for making this purchase?

Do I have a place to put it when I get it home?

How I Spend Money

Are you an A or a B?

1. A. I put money in a savings account.
    B. I scrounge money weekly with nothing left over for savings.

2. A. I only buy things after giving it much consideration.
    B. I buy something when I feel like it.

3. A. If I buy a major item, I compare prices, read up on the best product and then buy it.
    B. If I buy a major item, I go to a store and buy it, saving time by not comparing prices.

4. A. I prioritize leisure and spend money on it.
    B. I seldom spend money on leisure or entertainment.

5. A. I plan credit card purchases and pay the full balance when it is due.
    B. I overextend on credit cards, paying only part of the full balance each month.

6. A. I can control cash in my hand/wallet, or I make sure I never have cash "on hand."
    B. Cash burns a hole in my pocket and I must spend it if I have it.

7. A. I choose to spend some money on myself.
    B. I never spend money on myself.

8. A. I manage my money independently and do not ask others to help me out.
    B. I ask for help from those who can manage money better than I can.

9. A. I keep an eye on my financial situation, evaluating and updating my budget frequently.
    B. My money has a mind of its own and I allow my money to run itself.

10. A. I know my income, expenses and budget, and plan accordingly.
    B. I do not know my financial situation, so I do not plan.

What do you need to do to be in control of your money? _____
_____
_____
_____
_____

What are you going to do to help yourself do it? _____
_____
_____
_____
_____

My Budget Worksheet

	WEEK 1	WEEK 2	WEEK 3	WEEK 4
INCOME:				
Wages:	_____	_____	_____	_____
Payments:	_____	_____	_____	_____
Sales:	_____	_____	_____	_____

FIXED EXPENSES: (These are the same every month)

Rent/Mortgage:	_____	Insurance:	
Utilities:	_____	House	_____
Gas	_____	Car	_____
Electricity	_____		
Water/Sewer	_____	Loans:	_____
Garbage	_____		
Telephone	_____	Car Payment:	_____
Cable TV	_____		

VARIABLE EXPENSES: (These vary at times)

	WEEK 1	WEEK 2	WEEK 3	WEEK 4
Food	_____	_____	_____	_____
Clothing/shoes	_____	_____	_____	_____
Child care	_____	_____	_____	_____
Doctor	_____	_____	_____	_____
Dentist	_____	_____	_____	_____
Medicine	_____	_____	_____	_____
Treatments	_____	_____	_____	_____
Pet expenses	_____	_____	_____	_____
Car expenses	_____	_____	_____	_____
Gas/Oil	_____	_____	_____	_____
Maintenance	_____	_____	_____	_____
Entertainment	_____	_____	_____	_____
Cigarettes	_____	_____	_____	_____
Gambling	_____	_____	_____	_____
Hobbies/Crafts	_____	_____	_____	_____
Books/Magazines	_____	_____	_____	_____
Other	_____	_____	_____	_____
Weekly Totals:	_____	_____	_____	_____

You MUST budget and pay the fixed expenses every month. Never use the fixed expense money to pay the variable expenses. This is the roof over your head!

Compare your yearly costs by keeping this record

Monthly Record of Energy Use and Cost

YEAR	ELECTRICITY			GAS/OIL		WATER	
	Total Cost	kwh used		Total Cost	cu. Ft. use	Total Cost	gal/cu used
JAN							
FEB							
MAR							
APR							
MAY							
JUN							
JUL							
AUG							
SEP							
OCT							
NOV							
DEC							

Monthly Record of Energy Use and Cost

YEAR	ELECTRICITY			GAS/OIL		WATER	
	Total Cost	kwh used		Total Cost	cu. Ft. use	Total Cost	gal/cu used
JAN							
FEB							
MAR							
APR							
MAY							
JUN							
JUL							
AUG							
SEP							
OCT							
NOV							
DEC							

Baby-Sitting Expenses

Name: _____

Name of Sitter:	Date:	Time Spent/Hours:	Rate of Pay	Amount Paid:
_____	_____	_____	$_____	$_____
_____	_____	_____	$_____	$_____
_____	_____	_____	$_____	$_____
_____	_____	_____	$_____	$_____
_____	_____	_____	$_____	$_____
_____	_____	_____	$_____	$_____
_____	_____	_____	$_____	$_____
_____	_____	_____	$_____	$_____
_____	_____	_____	$_____	$_____
_____	_____	_____	$_____	$_____
_____	_____	_____	$_____	$_____
_____	_____	_____	$_____	$_____
_____	_____	_____	$_____	$_____
_____	_____	_____	$_____	$_____
_____	_____	_____	$_____	$_____
_____	_____	_____	$_____	$_____
_____	_____	_____	$_____	$_____
_____	_____	_____	$_____	$_____
_____	_____	_____	$_____	$_____

Total Hours: _____   Total Paid: $_____

Alimony/Support Payments

Name: _____

Amount Sent/Received	Date Sent/Received	Amount Past Due	Next Payment Due
$ _____	_____	$ _____	_____
$ _____	_____	$ _____	_____
$ _____	_____	$ _____	_____
$ _____	_____	$ _____	_____
$ _____	_____	$ _____	_____
$ _____	_____	$ _____	_____
$ _____	_____	$ _____	_____
$ _____	_____	$ _____	_____
$ _____	_____	$ _____	_____
$ _____	_____	$ _____	_____
$ _____	_____	$ _____	_____
$ _____	_____	$ _____	_____
$ _____	_____	$ _____	_____
$ _____	_____	$ _____	_____
$ _____	_____	$ _____	_____
$ _____	_____	$ _____	_____
$ _____	_____	$ _____	_____
$ _____	_____	$ _____	_____
$ _____	_____	$ _____	_____
$ _____	Total	$ _____	Total

Ways to Save Money

Hunt for local bargains:
Get copies of your local newspaper and look for sales and specials. Check the classified ads for items you need. Ask if the paper offers discount cards to subscribers. Read weekly supermarket circulars and plan meals based on the week's sales.

Cancel extra credit cards:
Only keep two cards—one for convenience and one for backup. Use cards with the lowest interest rates and no annual fees.

Find a good bank:
Shop around. Ask a few banks for a list of fees and other balance requirements, then compare. Pick a checking account with a minimum balance you can easily keep. Does opening a savings account make a checking account free, or at least cheaper? If you use ATM machines, use a bank with a no-fee machine where you shop. Credit unions usually provide bargains to their members. See if you qualify to join one.

Save much on electric bills:
Look around for lights that have 100-watt bulbs in them. Replace with 60-watt bulbs and save over the year. Also shut off the dishwasher before the dry cycle and let the dishes air dry.

Eat less fast food:
For 30 days, try not to eat out. If that is impossible, keep a record of how much you spend when buying fast food. Watch pop and coffees, too. They add up quickly.

Vacations:
Try camping. Look for family discounts when booking a hotel room. Always ask if prices are cut for membership in groups like AAA.

Cut back-to-school costs:
Take outgrown children's clothes to a thrift store, and shop for usable items. You may find friends and set up a trade group, or even order kid's clothes from an outlet store and split the shipping costs.

Hold a yard sale:
Getting rid of things you no longer need and use is helpful in many ways. Garage sales are busy at the beginning of summer, end of summer and even before Christmas when people are looking for Christmas gifts.

How are your skills?
Your skills can be a source of extra income. Do you sew? Crafts? There are other people who would willingly pay for you to help them out.

Winterize your home:
Don't pay to heat the outdoors! Look for cracks and leaks. Insulate and keep the thermostat low in winter.

Always keep looking for ways to cut costs. The money you save—you have really earned!

Long-Distance Phone Call Record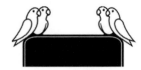

Date	Name of Caller	Party Called	Number Called	Time From	To
____	____	____	____	____	____
____	____	____	____	____	____
____	____	____	____	____	____
____	____	____	____	____	____
____	____	____	____	____	____
____	____	____	____	____	____
____	____	____	____	____	____
____	____	____	____	____	____
____	____	____	____	____	____
____	____	____	____	____	____
____	____	____	____	____	____
____	____	____	____	____	____
____	____	____	____	____	____
____	____	____	____	____	____
____	____	____	____	____	____
____	____	____	____	____	____
____	____	____	____	____	____
____	____	____	____	____	____

Traffic Violations Record

Name: _____   Date: _____

Tickets Received

Ticket # _____   Description:_____
Date: _____   Cost: $ _____   Points: _____

Ticket # _____   Description:_____
Date: _____   Cost: $ _____   Points: _____

Ticket # _____   Description:_____
Date: _____   Cost: $ _____   Points: _____

Ticket # _____   Description:_____
Date: _____   Cost: $ _____   Points: _____

Ticket # _____   Description:_____
Date: _____   Cost: $ _____   Points: _____

Total Points:_____

Defensive Driving Courses Taken: _____   Date: _____
Reason: _____
_____

License Suspension/Revocation: _____   Date began: _____   Date Ended: _____
Reason: _____
_____

Additional Traffic-Related Charges: _____
_____

Additional Information: _____
_____

Funeral Planning Guide

Name of Deceased: _____

Funeral Home: _____

Address: _____

Funeral Plan: _____

Director: _____ Phone: _____

Type of Service:

     Religious _____ Military_____ Fraternal _____

Officiator: _____

Music Selections: _____

Reading Selections: _____

Flowers: _____

Memorials: _____

Pallbearers: _____

Disposition of Remains

Burial: Name of Cemetery: _____

Location: _____

     Section: _____ Plot #: _____ Block: _____

Deed Location: _____

Other Instructions: _____

_____

Cremation: Disposition of Ashes: _____

Cremation performed at: _____

Other Instructions: _____

Coverage of Funeral Expenses

Life Insurance: _____

Burial Insurance: _____ Fraternal Organizations: _____

Social Security: _____ Veterans Administration: _____

Pension Benefit: _____

Union Benefit: _____

Teaching Your Children the Value of Money

Money does not grow on trees. You need to start teaching your children about money by the time they are two years old. They see you take money out and pay the store clerk and they know that it is called "money." They want some, too. You can set a small amount for a very young child, like a dime or a quarter, and have them put the coin in their pocket when you go to the store. You can point out items that would be possible for them to buy with that coin.

As your children start school, they may request an allowance. This is where questions arise. Do you pay the children an allowance for doing chores around the house? Do you pay for extra work done? How much do you pay? Much depends on what your ability to pay is. Children need to learn that they are a necessary part of the family and must do things around the house because they live there, too. Should children be paid to get good grades in school? These questions depend on your family values. When children want money, they should realize that they will need to do something to earn at least a part of it. They also should be taught from the beginning to save a portion of the money they earn also. Even young children can learn to invest their money and watch it grow.

By the time your children get into the teen years, it is very necessary that they know what a budget is and can keep one for themselves. Parents can put a foundation sum for clothing and have their teen earn the money they spend over that bottom line for clothes they want. If you suspect your children are experimenting with drugs, alcohol and sex, then you must tighten the money belt. If children are going to engage in adult behavior, they must be fully responsible as adults, which means earning every penny they need. Parents who always hand out money to their children without responsibility make children helpless on their own.

Raise your children to be independent and self-sufficient. You will be very proud and they will be proud, too!

Health and Fitness

SECTION
4

My Health and Fitness Records

Your health and fitness is not something to be considered at a time when you are ill. Unfortunately, we never think about it while we are young. Then, comes along a time when we say to ourselves, "This time I've got to: quit smoking, lose weight, get a better night's sleep, find more energy, etc." Where do you stand in this area right now? Are you satisfied with your physical condition?

Physical Fitness:

How is your balance?

How is your flexibility?

How is your muscular strength?

How is your muscular endurance?

How is your cardio-respiratory endurance and   stamina?

General Health and Well-Being:

Do you need weight control?

Do you need body shape and tone adjustment?

How is your digestion?

Do you get adequate sleep and rest?

Do you need more energy and enthusiasm?

This section is to record where you are presently and help you keep records of where you wish to go. You may also find these records helpful if you need medical assistance so that your Doctor can have a historical perspective on your condition. You might wish to take a class or workshop on stress reduction. Be sure to include how that helps you in the way you feel. You may wish to join a health club, and by keeping records on your progress, you can see what is most effective for you. You may want to go to a weight loss clinic. Add any records that you feel will help you keep in control of your own health and fitness. Health and fitness is another piece in your total successful life plan.

What Stress Can Make You Sick?

Did you know that stress could cause you to be ill, cause accidents, or cause even death? What are some stressors that come up in everyone's life? Here is a list of common stressors. Check off events which have happened to you within the last year and total up the score. A score of 150 would make your chances of developing an illness or a health change about 50-50. A score of 300 gives a chance of a health change of almost 90%.

Death of a spouse/partner ...... 100 points	Son or daughter leaving home 30
Divorce 75	Trouble with in-laws 30
Marital separation 65	Outstanding personal achievement 30
Jail/prison term 65	Spouse begins or stops work 25
Death of a close family member 65	Change in living conditions 25
Personal injury or serious illness 55	Starting or finishing school 25
Marriage 50	Revision of personal habits 25
Fired from work 50	Trouble with boss 25
Marital reconciliation 45	Change in work hours or conditions 20
Retirement 45	Change in residence 20
Change in family member's health 45	Change in schools 20
Pregnancy 40	Change in recreational habits 20
Sexual difficulties 40	Change in church activities 20
Addition to family 40	Change in social activities 20
Business readjustment 40	Mortgage or loan under $10,000 15
Change in financial status 40	Change in sleeping habits 15
Death of a close friend 35	Change in number of family gatherings 15
Change to a different line of work 35	Change in eating habits 15
Change in number of marital arguments 35	Vacation 10
Mortgage or loan over $10,000 30	Christmas season 10
Foreclosure of mortgage or loan 30	Minor violation of the law 10
Change in work responsibilities 30	Total score: _____

Is your score an accurate indication of the stress in your life? What should you do?

Medical Records

The purpose of maintaining your medical health records is so that, in case of an emergency, you have the immediate information available to assist in your care.

Each family member should have his or her own record maintained and quickly available in case of need.

My Health History

Name _____   Date of Birth _____

Place of birth _____   Doctor _____

Sex   F_____   M_____   Height _____   Weight _____

Special circumstances (if any) surrounding my birth_____
_____
_____
_____

My blood type and Rh factor _____

Identifying marks or scars_____
_____
_____

Major illnesses, accidents and operations:

Age	Date	What happened?	Doctor	Outcome

Record of X-Rays

Date	Type of X-ray	Taken at	For the Reason

Record of Allergic Reactions

Record allergic reactions! Any reaction can be more severe and can be fatal.

Date	Age	Reaction to	Type of Treatment	Outcome

Hospitalization Records

1. Name: _____

Date of Hospitalization: _____ to _____

Name of Hospital: _____ Phone: _____

Location: _____

Reason for Hospitalization: _____

_____

Treatment: _____

Attending Physician: _____

Address: _____ Phone: _____

Hospitalization Costs: $ _____

Comments: _____

_____

2. Name: _____

Date of Hospitalization: _____ to _____

Name of Hospital: _____ Phone: _____

Location: _____

Reason for Hospitalization: _____

_____

Treatment: _____

Attending Physician: _____

Address: _____ Phone: _____

Hospitalization Costs: $ _____

Comments: _____

_____

3. Name: _____

Date of Hospitalization: _____ to _____

Name of Hospital: _____ Phone: _____

Location: _____

Reason for Hospitalization: _____

_____

Treatment: _____

Attending Physician: _____

Address: _____ Phone: _____

Hospitalization Costs: $ _____

Comments: _____

_____

Conditions affecting my immediate blood relatives

☐ Anemia	☐ Cancer	☐ Glaucoma	☐ Kidney disease
☐ Aneurysm	☐ Cystic fibrosis	☐ Heart Disease	☐ Multiple sclerosis
☐ Arthritis	☐ Diabetes	☐ Hemophilia	☐ Muscular dystrophy
☐ Asthma	☐ Down's syndrome	☐ Hypertension	☐ Parkinson's disease
☐ Arteriosclerosis	☐ Epilepsy	☐ Hypoglycemia	☐ Scoliosis

Personal Medical Profile:

Immunized against:

☐ DIP (diphtheria, tetanus, and pertussis)

☐ Mumps ☐ Polio ☐ Rubella (German measles)

☐ Measles ☐ Smallpox ☐ Hib (meningitis)

☐ Hepatitus B

Diseases contracted:

Childhood

☐ Chicken pox ☐ Measles ☐ Mumps ☐ Polio

☐ Rubella (German measles) ☐ Hepatitis ☐ Malaria

Adult

☐ Tuberculosis ☐ STDs (Sexually transmitted)

☐ Other _____

Permanent problems and conditions: _____

_____

_____

Organ Donor Program

Representative: _____

Address: _____

_____

Phone: _____

Signed _____

MEDICAL HISTORY: Check correct box below for each question. Please do not skip any questions.

DO YOU HAVE A HISTORY OR CONTINUING PROBLEM WITH THE FOLLOWING?

YES	NO		YES	NO		YES	NO	
☐	☐	Migraines	☐	☐	Asthma	☐	☐	Suicidal thoughts
☐	☐	Ear ringing	☐	☐	Short of breath	☐	☐	Depression
☐	☐	Ear infections	☐	☐	Thyroid disease	☐	☐	Anxiety/fears
☐	☐	Bad vision	☐	☐	Back pain	☐	☐	Mental illness
☐	☐	Double vision	☐	☐	Rashes	☐	☐	Hemorrhoids
☐	☐	Eye infections	☐	☐	Heart murmur	☐	☐	High blood pressure
☐	☐	Nosebleeds	☐	☐	Heart attack	☐	☐	Blood in urine
☐	☐	Sinus trouble	☐	☐	Heart irregular	☐	☐	Frequent urination
☐	☐	Sore throat	☐	☐	Swollen ankles	☐	☐	Gall bladder disease
☐	☐	Allergies	☐	☐	Diarrhea	☐	☐	Kidney disease
☐	☐	Hoarseness	☐	☐	Constipation	☐	☐	Fainting
☐	☐	Cancer	☐	☐	Stroke	☐	☐	Emphysema
☐	☐	Convulsions	☐	☐	Broken bones	☐	☐	Arthritis
☐	☐	Blood clots	☐	☐	Bloody stools	☐	☐	Hernia
☐	☐	Pneumonia	☐	☐	Bronchitis	☐	☐	Anemia
☐	☐	Diabetes	☐	☐	Stroke	☐	☐	Tuberculosis

Regularly used prescriptions

Rx: _____ for _____ by Doctor: _____

Rx: _____ for _____ by Doctor: _____

Rx: _____ for _____ by Doctor: _____

Rx: _____ for _____ by Doctor: _____

Rx: _____ for _____ by Doctor: _____

Rx: _____ for _____ by Doctor: _____

Rx: _____ for _____ by Doctor: _____

Power of Attorney for Health Care

1. **DESIGNATION OF HEALTH CARE AGENT:**

I, _____
   (Principal)

Hereby appoint:_____
   (Attorney-in-fact's name)

_____

(Access and phone number
as my attorney-in-fact (or Agent) to make health and personal care decisions for me as authorized in this document.

2. **EFFECTIVE DATE AND DURABILITY:** By this document, I intend to create a durable power of attorney effective upon, and only during, any period of incapacity in which, in the opinion of my agent and attending physician, I am unable to make or communicate a choice regarding a particular health- care decision.

3. **AGENT'S POWERS:** I grant to my Agent full authority to make decisions for me regarding my health care. In exercising this authority, my Agent shall follow my desires as stated in this document or otherwise known to my Agent. In making any decision, my Agent shall attempt to discuss the proposed decision with me to determine my desires if I am able to communicate in any way. If my
Agent cannot determine the choice I would want made, then my Agent shall make a choice for me based upon what my Agent believes to be in my best interests. My Agent's authority to interpret my desires is intended to be as broad as possible, except for any limitations I may state below. Accordingly, unless specifically limited by Section 4, below, my Agent is authorized as follows:

   A. To consent, refuse, or withdraw consent to any and all types of medical care, treatment, surgical procedures, diagnostic procedures, medication, and the use of mechanical or other procedures that affect any bodily function, including (but not limited to) artificial respiration, nutritional support and hydration, and cardiopulmonary resuscitation;

   B. To have access to medical records and information to the same extent that I am entitled to, including the right to disclose the contents to others;

   C. To authorize my admission to or discharge (even against medical advice) from any hospital, nursing home, residential care, assisted living or similar facility or service;

   D. To contract on my behalf for any health-care related service or facility on my behalf, without my Agent incurring personal financial liability for such contracts;

   E. To hire and fire medical, social service, and other support personnel responsible for my care;

   F. To authorize, or refuse to authorize, any medication or procedure intended to relieve pain, even though such use may lead to physical damage, addiction, or hasten the moment of (but not intentionally cause) my death;

   G. To make anatomical gifts of part or all of my body for medical purposes, authorize an autopsy, and direct the disposition of my remains, to the extent permitted by law:

   H. To take any other action necessary to do what I authorize here, including (but not limited to) granting any waiver or release from liability required by any hospital, physician, or other health-care provider; signing any documents relating to refusals of treatment or the leaving of a facility against medical advice, and pursuing any legal action in my name, and at the expense of my estate to force compliance with my wishes as determined by my Agent, or to seek actual or punitive damages for the failure to comply.

      a. The powers granted above do not include the following powers or are subject to the following rules or limitations:

4. **STATEMENT OF DESIRES, SPECIAL PROVISIONS, AND LIMITATIONS:**

_____

_____

b.   With respect to any Life-Sustaining Treatment, I direct the following: (initial only one of the following paragraphs)

☐ **REFERENCE TO LIVING WILL.** I specifically direct my Agent to follow any health-care declaration or "living will" executed by me.

☐ **GRANT TO DISCRETION TO AGENT.** I do not want my life to be prolonged nor do I want life-sustaining treatment to be provided or continued if my Agent believes the burdens of the treatment outweigh the expected benefits. I want my Agent to consider the relief of suffering, the expense involved and the quality as well as the possible extension of my life in making decisions concerning life-sustaining treatment.

☐ **DIRECTIVE TO WITHHOLD OR WITHDRAW TREATMENT.** I do not want my life to be prolong and i do not want life-sustaining treatment:

☐   A. If I have a condition that is incurable or irreversible and, without the administration of life-sustaining treatment, expected to result in death withing a relatively short time; or

☐   B. If I am in a coma or persistent vegetative state, which is reasonable, concluded to be irreversible.

☐ **DIRECTIVE FOR MAXIMUM TREATMENT.** I want my life to be prolonged to the greatest extent possible without regard to my condition, the chances I have for recovery, or the cost of the procedures.

☐ **DIRECTIVE IN MY OWN WORDS.**

_____

_____

_____

☐   C. With respect to Nutrition and Hydration provided by means of a nasogastric tube or tube into the stomach, intestines, or veins, I wish to make clear that…
(Initial only one)

☐   I intend to include these procedures among the {life-sustaining procedures" that may be withheld or withdrawn under the conditions given above.

☐   I do not intend to include these procedures among the "life-sustaining procedures" that may be withheld or withdrawn.

5. **SUCCESSORS:** If any Agent named by me shall die, become legally disabled, resign, refuse to act, be unavailable, or (if any Agent is my spouse) be legally separated or divorced from me, I name the following (each to act alone and successively, in the order named) as successors to my Agent:

a.   First Alternate Agent_____
Address: _____

b.   Second Alternate Agent_____
Address: _____

6. **PROTECTION OF THIRD PARTIES WHO RELY ON MY AGENT:** No person who relies in good faith upon any representations by my Agent or Successor Agent shall be liable to me, my estate, my heirs or assigns, for recognizing the Agent's authority.

7. **NOMINATION OF GUARDIAN**: If a guardian of my person should for any reason be appointed, I nominate my Agent (or his/her successor), named above.

8. **ADMINISTRATIVE PROVISIONS:**

    a. I revoke any prior power of attorney for health care.

    b. This power of attorney is intended to be valid in any jurisdiction in which it is presented.

    c. My Agent shall not be entitled to compensation for services performed under this power of attorney, but he or she shall be entitled to reimbursement for all reasonable expenses incurred as a result of carrying out any provision of this power of attorney.

    d. The powers delegated under this power of attorney are separable, so that the invalidity of one or more powers shall not affect any others.

BY SIGNING HERE, I INDICATE THAT I UNDERSTAND THE CONTENTS OF THIS DOCUMENT AND THE EFFECT OF THIS GRANT OF POWERS TO MY AGENT.

I sign my name to this Health Care Power of Attorney on this _____ **day of** _____(Month), 20 _____.

Signature: _____

Print name: _____

Address: _____

Witness statement: I declare that the person who signed or acknowledged this document is personally known to me, that he/she signed or acknowledged this durable power of attorney in my presence, and that he/she appears to be of sound mind and under no duress, fraud, or undue influence. I am not the person appointed as Agent by this document, nor am I the patient's health-care provider, or an employee of the patient's health-care provider. I further declare that I am not related to the principal by blood, marriage, or adoption, and, to the best of my knowledge, I am not a creditor of the principal nor entitled to any part of his/her estate under a will now existing or by operation of law.

Witness #1:

Signature _____   Date: _____

Print name: _____

Address: _____   Phone: _____

Witness #2:

Signature _____   Date: _____

Print name: _____

Address: _____   Phone: _____

NOTARIZATION

STATE OF _____

County of _____

On this _____ day of _____, 20_____, the said _____, known to me (or satisfactorily proven) to be the person named in the foregoing instrument, personally appeared before me, a Notary Public, within and for the State and County aforesaid, and acknowledged that he or she freely and voluntarily executed the same for the purposes stated therein.

My Commission Expires:

_____   _____
                                                                           Notary Public

My Child's Immunization Record

Schedule of immunizations:

For (Child's Name) _____

At Age	*Type of Inoculation*
2 months	DPT (diptheria-pertussis-tetanus), OPV (oral polio vaccine)
4 months	DPT, OPV
6 months	DPT, OPV
1 year	Tuberculin test
15 months	MMR (measles-mumps-rubella)
18 months	18 months HbCv (haemophilius influenza type b conjugated vaccine.) OPV
4 to 6 years	DPT, OPV
14 to 16 years	Td (tetanus – diptheria)
every 10 years	Td

Record the date given and child's reactions to the vaccines such as fever, irritability, redness or tenderness where the shot was given.

Date: Reaction:

_____   _____

_____   _____

_____   _____

_____   _____

_____   _____

Special Notes:

Child's Health Record

(Keep a separate health record on each member of the family)

Child's name: _____   Date of Birth: _____   Sex: _____

Health History: Has your child had any of the problems below?

1. Allergies or reactions (to food, medication or other) .... Yes _____   No _____
2. Hay fever, asthma, or wheezing.. Yes _____   No _____
3. Eczema or frequent skin rashes .... Yes _____   No _____
4. Convulsion or seizures... Yes _____   No _____
5. Heart trouble.. Yes _____   No _____
6. Diabetes... Yes _____   No _____
7. Frequent colds, sore throats, earaches (4 or more per year) .... Yes _____   No _____
8. Trouble with passing urine or bowel movements....................... Yes _____   No _____
9. Shortness of breath.. Yes _____   No _____
10. Speech problems.. Yes _____   No _____
10. Menstrual problems .... Yes _____   No _____
12. Dental problems... Yes _____   No _____
13 Other problems .... Yes _____   No _____

Does your child take medication regularly? .... Yes _____   No _____

Reason for medication _____

Yearly Physical

Child's weight:_____lbs. Height : _____ ft. ___inches   Child's weight: _____lbs. Height : _____ ft.___inches

Date: _____   Date _____

Date: _____   Date _____

Date: _____   Date _____

Date: _____   Date _____

Date: _____   Date _____

Tests and Measurements:

Test Type and Date Tested

Vision _____   ☐ visual acuity   ☐ ocular muscle   ☐ other

Hearing _____   ☐ Audiometer   ☐ Other

Hemoglobin/hematocrit_____

Urinalysis _____   ☐ sugar   ☐ albumin   ☐ microscopic

Blood Pressure _____

Tuberculin _____   Result: ☐ Positive   ☐ Negative

Family Medicine Cabinet

Review   Check your medicine cabinet contents
Check all expiration dates
Read all labels and check warnings
Make a list of any concerns or questions you may have for your doctor or pharmacist

Remove   All expired medicines
All OTC (over the counter) and prescription medicines you no longer take
All children's medicines that no longer have dosing instructions or dosing devices

For Pain and Fever

For effective temporary relief of pain and fever:

☐ Acetaminophen – for fever and minor aches and pains of colds and flu, minor arthritis pain, toothache and backache.

☐ Ibuprofen – for muscle aches, headache, colds and flue and fever.

☐ Thermometer – to take temperature.

☐ Sterile gauze pads

Wound Care

☐ Adhesive bandages

☐ Rubbing alcohol

☐ Antibiotic ointment

☐ Cotton swabs

☐ Cotton balls

☐ Elastic bandages

☐ Tweezers for removing thorns and splinters

☐ Ice bag for use on minor sprains to reduce swelling

☐ Hot water bag or heating pad for muscle pain

Heartburn/acid indigestion

To relieve and prevent heartburn and acid indigestion:

☐ Antacids – to neutralize stomach acid and relieve heartburn.

☐ Acid Reducers— to control acid production to prevent and relieve heartburn.

Allergy and Sinus

For the relief of allergy symptoms, sinusitis, congestion and sinus headache:

☐ Antihistamine—for relief of sneezing, runny nose, and itching.

☐ Decongestant – for stuffy nose.

☐ Pain Reliever – for sinus pain and pressure.

Watch for possible side effects, as drowsiness, from antihistamines.

Colds and Flue

For the symptoms of colds and flu:

☐ Antihistamine – for relief of sneezing, runny nose, and itching.

☐ Decongestant – for stuffy nose.

☐ Antitussive – to relieve a dry cough.

☐ Expectorant – to loosen a cough.

☐ Thermometer for temperature.

Diarrhea

To control the symptoms of diarrhea:

☐ Anti-Diarrheal

To control the symptoms of diarrhea plus bloating, pressure and cramps, commonly referred to as gas.

☐ Anti-Diarrheal + Anti-Gas.

Poisoning

Call your local poison control center before inducing vomiting. Some poisons should not be vomited.

☐ Syrup of Ipecac

You can help prevent the spread of illness!

Good Health habits are vital in preventing the spread of disease. Teach your children to have good habits too.

- Wash your hands before you eat. Do not bite your fingernails.
- Wash your hands after using the toilet
- Do not share common personal items such as spoons, forks, cups or glasses, combs, towels and food.
- Keep your fingernails and toenails clean and trimmed
- Always cover your mouth when coughing or sneezing.
- Stay home when you are sick, and avoid others when they are ill.
- Do not chew or bite on objects like toys or pencils.

The kitchen and the bathroom are the two rooms that need daily cleaning to prevent disease. You can inspect your kitchen and take steps to prevent contamination of food prepared there.

There are five very dangerous strains of bacteria that are found in the food supply. How sick you get depends on which bacteria you ingest, how much you ingest, and how strong your immune system is. Children are at a higher risk of getting ill, as are pregnant women, elderly persons and persons who have a chronic illness. No one likes to be sick with food poisoning! General symptoms are diarrhea, which may show blood, stomach pain, fever, nausea and vomiting, headache and chills.

- Campylobacter is a bacteria in raw chicken, undercooked meat, poultry and shellfish, untreated water, unpasteurized milk.
- Salmonella is a bacteria found in undercooked or improperly refrigerated meat, poultry, stuffing, eggs, unpasteurized milk. Ice cream can be contaminated. Only cooking at temperatures over 165° F can kill these bacteria.
- Clostridium perfringens is found in undercooked meat and poultry, foods left too long on an under heated table or counter.
- Staphylococcus aureus is found in improperly refrigerated meat and dairy products, pasta and potato salads, custards and cream-filled desserts.
- Clostridium botulinus is found in home-canned foods or damaged cans and containers of low-acid foods, food kept in conditions of limited oxygen such as a foil-wrapped potato left out overnight. This can be fatal!

Safe Storage Tips:

1. Refrigerator must be 40° F or below and the freezer 0∞ F or below. Use a thermometer to check. The sooner food is chilled the less chance for bacteria to grow.

2. Keep refrigerator clean and orderly, allowing cool air to circulate freely so the temperature remains even throughout.

3. Do not put uncovered food into the refrigerator where bacteria in the air can settle.

4. Do not store leftovers without dating them. Leftover meat stored in the refrigerator should not be used after three or four days.

5. You can't always depend on your eyes and nose to tell you if a food is safe, but you should get rid of some things based on looks and odor alone:

   • Cracked eggs may contain salmonella. Keep eggs in their original carton, which can protect them from cracks, on a shelf in the refrigerator.

   • Dented, bulging or rusty cans may harbor bacteria

   • Jars with loose or cracked lids, especially those containing milky liquids that are normally clear is a sign of the botulism toxin and very dangerous.

   • A jar of mayonnaise or tub of margarine harboring bits of other foods, such as toast crumbs, may be contaminated.

   • Sliced or peeled fruit or vegetables left un-refrigerated and uncovered for more than a few hours can allow bacteria to enter.

   • Bread or cheese with green mold may be toxic.

   • Anything that looks suspect, such as gray-looking meat or fish with an off odor. "When in doubt, throw it out!"

Look at the Pantry:

Keep the dry foods in tightly closed boxes, opened bags of flour and sugar in re-sealable plastic bags, tightly closed bottles, and clean conditions in a cool, dry, dark location. None of the cans should be dented or bulging – warning signs of bacterial contamination. Store the food in cabinets and not under the sink, where dampness can encourage bacterial growth and molds. Keep cleaning supplies away from the food storage also.

Check your countertops:

Try to work with only one perishable food at a time and wash the counter or cutting board and utensils with hot soapy water between foods and at the finish. Washing your hands with soap and water after handling any uncooked food is best. Using cutting boards can save the countertop, but juices from meats can get into cuts and scratches. Be sure to wash any cutting board thoroughly and pour boiling water over it periodically.

Cooking Safely:

To make sure any food is cooked thoroughly, you should set your oven temperature at 325° F or higher. Never taste meat, poultry or seafood while it's raw or before it is fully cooked. Cook meat that is less that 2 inches thick until the center is no longer pink and the juice is clear, not bloody. Hamburger is especially likely to contain dangerous bacteria because the grinding process can spread contaminants throughout the meat. Another danger zone is turkey with stuffing. Stuff the turkey just before roasting. Once it is cooked, remove the stuffing from the turkey and store it in the refrigerator.

Microwave cooking does not heat foods evenly. Cold spots in a food may harbor dangerous bacteria and hot spots can cause burns. Let food stand for up to five minutes after you have cooked it to allow the temperature to even out.

Cleaning Safely:

Small appliances, utensils and dishes can transfer bacteria to food if not properly cleaned or cared for, such as cracked dishes. Can openers should have no food particles clinging to the blade. Check cleanliness of the blender and be sure all parts are thoroughly clean before using.

Scrub the sink down along with the countertops, after you work with raw poultry, meat or fish. Remember bacteria thrive on water and food, so anytime a sponge contains food debris and is left sitting in water, you are encouraging bacterial growth. It is a good idea to clean countertops and sinks with a detergent containing bleach, which kills harmful bacteria. Even dishwashers, should be checked for cleanliness.

Garbage and Trash:

Do not let garbage and trash sit out to draw flies and other pests. You can compost most vegetable garbage in the garden. Meat, fish and bones must be discarded carefully so that pets do not get into them. They are not to be placed in the compost either. You can bury them if you put them deep into the ground. You may wish to recycle the majority of your trash and you can do this easily if you organize the various kinds of materials to recycle and find boxes or bins to place the recyclables in. Aluminum cans, plastic bottles, foam cups, should be rinsed out clean and flattened if possible. Paper and cardboard can be tied into bundles. Garbage must be in a covered container as it draws disease and pests and should be disposed of as soon as possible. If you deal with your garbage correctly, you should have no odor problem.

When to Use the Emergency Room

Reasons to go to the Emergency Room:

1. If person is unconscious
2. Has really bad pain
3. Has difficulty breathing
4. Is bleeding badly
5. Has had poisoning
6. Has a major injury, such as a head injury

NOT very good reasons for an Emergency room visit:

1. Colds, cough, sore throat, flu. You can see your Doctor.
2. Rash
3. Moderate fever
4. Ordinary earache
5. Possible sprain
6. Possible broken bone, unless bone is showing or very distorted
7. Small cut or dog bite with controlled bleeding.

You should have information on how to care for the sick at home. In case of accidents, you can call for information if you need it. You may wish to take courses on CPR, first aid, or other information to help you be prepared in emergencies. Contact your local health department for additional information.

Staying healthy means you are in control of your medical records, medications and information and can work together with your Doctor to maintain your health.

You and Your Doctor

When you see the Doctor:

1. Have a list of questions that you wish to have answered.

2. Tell the truth. If you are taking other over the counter medicines, be sure the Doctor knows this to tell you of possible side effects or conflicts with medicine prescribed.

3. Leave family and friends in the waiting room. While support is nice, you need to talk to the Doctor alone and address all the present issues you have. Take notes to remember what you are told. Be sure you understand what recommendations the Doctor is making to you.

4. Know your medicines. Learn the names and dosages of all drugs you take and make sure every Doctor you see has a complete list of both prescribed and over-the-counter remedies. Some drugs can interact dangerously with another drug, a food, or other substances. Be particularly careful if you take drugs for glaucoma, diabetes, hypertension or abnormal heartbeat.

   - What will this medicine do for me?
   - Does this drug have side effects?
   - Will the medication interfere with other drugs I am taking?
   - Should I avoid this drug if I am ill?
   - What if I'm pregnant?
   - Can I change the dosage?
   - What times of the day should I take this drug?
   - Can I share this medication?
   - Can I substitute a generic drug?

5. Take care of yourself. You are responsible for your own health and safety. Doctors can help you, but not if you play games and do not take seriously what the recommendations are. If you need to lose weight, eat healthy, exercise and reduce stress and show that you are serious about your own health.

6. Remember Doctors are very busy. If you are late to appointments, or otherwise do not respect the professional time given to you, do not expect to get favored treatment.

Choosing a Doctor/Dentist/Specialist/Therapist

Name _____   Specialty _____

Address _____   Phone (____) _____
          Travel time from Home _____minutes

Referred by _____   Phone (____) _____

Address _____

Degree in _____   Certified by _____

Member of American Medical Association   ☐ Yes   ☐ No

Other membership _____

Hospital affiliation _____   Position: _____

Address _____
          Travel time from Home _____minutes

Medical school faculty   ☐ Yes   ☐ No   Position: _____

    Practice: Number of years _____   In this community/neighborhood_____

    Office hours: Weekdays _____   Days off: _____   Weekends_____

    How far in advance to make an appointment:_____

    Makes house calls   ☐ Yes   ☐ No   Usually prescribes generic drugs   ☐ Yes   ☐ No

Private practice: Support staff __ nurses_____   technicians _____

        On site: x-ray __ Lab _____   ambulatory surgery_____

        Referrals during weekends, vacations, and for surgery:

        Doctor: _____   Phone_____

        Address: _____

Specialized services : _____

Standard Fees: Consultation $ _____ Check-up $ _____ Office visit $_____

        If physical or mental therapist $_____ per session of _____ minutes.

Payment policy: Accepts Union plans _____ Medicare/Medicaid _____

        Prefers to bill patient directly for all fees and items:

        Requests payment ☐ at end of visit ☐ cash only ☐ personal check ☐ Sends statement

        Prefers to bill patient's insurance company for covered fees and items

        For fees not covered: requests payment
        ☐ at end of visit ☐ cash only ☐ personal check ☐ Sends statementYour Evaluation:

Your Evaluation

1. Do you feel comfortable with him/her? _____

2. Do you feel you can discuss most medical matters with him/her? _____

3. Have you discussed the living will choices? _____

4. Do you feel your views on extraordinary life-preserving measures are respected? _____

5. Will the Doctor honor your "living will" _____

6. In your opinion, the Doctor's strongest asset is _____

    The Doctor's weakest drawback is _____

    Office: Is the waiting room pleasant? _____ Very crowded with patients ? _____

7. Is the examination room pleasant? _____ uncomfortable? _____

8. Does the equipment seem up-to-date and well cared for? _____

9. Does the staff seem professional and courteous?_____

Keep Your Own Medical Records:

Most people visit different doctors over a lifetime. No one doctor can keep track of what the other specialists are doing or what medicines they are prescribing. If you fill out your health forms, keep the information up to date, and give a copy to your doctor, it will save time, and keep the information timely. You may also want to keep a copy in your suitcase when you travel, in case of an emergency. Having a record at hand can speed diagnosis and reduce the chance of duplicating expensive tests which have been done previously. It can serve as a handy inoculation record, so you can make sure you have all the necessary shots when you travel. If you are hospitalized, make sure you get a copy of the discharge summary, which gives the doctor's final assessment of your condition and keep with your medical records file in your important papers box. Also get all pathology and lab reports as well as copies of pertinent X-rays.

- Keep a file of all medications you take, prescriptions and over-the-counter, and show this to the pharmacist. He or she can spot possible drug problems and avoid adverse interactions.

- Keep copies of medical, hospital and pharmacy bills even if you are insured. These documents can be used to challenge insurance company rulings or inadequate reimbursement by Medicare.

- Consult family members to build a comprehensive medical history about yourself and other close relatives. Note family longevity patterns on both sides of your family as well as any history of diseases such as diabetes, cancer, high blood pressure, emphysema, alcoholism, heart disease and dementia.

- Call your doctor's office and work with staff there to complete your medical records if there are portions you are unsure how to answer. Ask them to send copies of important evaluations or tests.

Healthy Teeth and Gums

We all have lots of excuses why we don't brush three times a day and floss at night, but it's never too late to start good dental health habits. And like all habits, once you start, they'll soon become part of your daily routine. Try these suggestions for taking better care of your teeth:

- Use a good quality toothbrush with soft, end-rounded bristles and change it every two-to-three months (or sooner if the bristles get worn or bent).

- Use a toothpaste with fluoride and ask your dentist if you should use one with tartar control.

- Keep a toothbrush and toothpaste at work so you can brush after lunch.

- Make flossing part of your nighttime routine. If you have children, they should be flossing by the time they are eight or nine.

- What you eat also affects your dental health. Chew only sugarless gum and try to stay away from sugary candy. Sucking on hard candy is like giving your teeth a bath in sugar, so if you do, try to brush afterward.

- Follow your dentist's recommendations on prevention if you tend to be susceptible to dental disease. Developing good habits now to help prevent cavities and gum disease will keep your teeth, gums and mouth healthy for a natural smile.

My Dental History

Include those incidents that may have affected the way your teeth have grown, such as accidents that knocked a tooth out, thumb sucking, poor dietary habits, poor hygiene, etc.

At age:	What happened	Dentist	Outcome

Record of My Dental Visits

Date:	Work Done	Cost

Keeping Track of Weight Loss

Days	1	2	3	4	5	6	7	8	9	10	11	12	13	14	15	16	17	18	19	20	21	22	23	24	25	26	27	28	29	30	31
250																															
245																															
240																															
235																															
230																															
225																															
220																															
215																															
210																															
205																															
200																															
195																															
190																															
185																															
180																															
175																															
170																															
165																															
160																															
155																															
150																															
145																															
140																															
135																															
130																															
125																															
120																															
115																															
110																															
105																															
100																															
95																															
90																															
85																															
80																															
75																															
70																															
65																															

My Health and Fitness Plan

Goal I want to accomplish: _____

_____

By Date: _____

What will be my rewards for reaching this goal? _____

_____

_____

_____

What must I do to reach my goal: by date: _____

1. _____   _____

2. _____   _____

3. _____   _____

4. _____   _____

5. _____   _____

6. _____   _____

7. _____   _____

8. _____   _____

9. _____   _____

10. _____   _____

I can do this!

Your Family Disaster Plan

Fire   Flood   Accident   Earthquake   Severe Storm   High Winds

Disaster can happen at any time and any place and can be totally unexpected and can be devastating to you and your family unless you have taken steps to plan for action ahead of time.

You can prepare by talking about your plan with your family. First, you need to know what kind of disasters could happen in your community. Call the Red Cross or your local emergency management to find out what type of disaster is most likely to happen, such as earthquake, flood, hurricane, tornado, etc. Request information on how to prepare for it. Also, find out if your community has a warning signal, what it sounds like, and what you should do if you hear it. Ask about animal care because your pets may not be allowed inside an emergency shelter due to health regulations. Find out how to help elderly or disabled persons if needed. Also find out emergency plans at work and at your child's school or daycare center.

Then you need to have a family meeting to make your own family plans in case of a disaster. Discuss what types of disasters are most likely to happen and what each person should do in each case. Have a place to meet. In case of a house fire, plan a place outside where everyone can meet in safety. If you are not at home, where can you meet in case you cannot go back home? Everyone should know the address and phone number. You could ask a friend who lives far away to be your family contact, so those family members can call this person and tell them where they are. Plan how to take care of your pets.

Post emergency phone numbers by phones: fire, police, ambulance, and safe friend. Teach children how and when to call 911, or your local emergency team. Show family members how to shut off the water, gas and electricity at the main switches. Teach family members how to use the fire extinguisher in case it is needed. Stock emergency supplies and a Disaster Supplies kit. Determine the best escape routes from your home. Find two ways out of each room. Find safe spots in your home for other disasters, like tornado, hurricane, or high winds if you cannot leave the home.

Practice and maintain your plan by going through it every six months with your children. You may also want to meet with your neighbors and plan how the neighborhood could work together after a disaster until help arrives. Do a home hazard hunt with your children. During a disaster, ordinary objects in your home can cause injury or damage. Anything that can move, fall, break or cause a fire is a home hazard. Bookshelves can fall over, hot water heaters can burst, and gas lines can break.

If a disaster strikes, follow instructions of local emergency officials. Wear protective clothing and sturdy shoes, take your disaster supplies kit, lock your home, and use travel routes specified by local authorities because certain areas may be impassable or dangerous. If you have time, shut off water and electricity before leaving. Note: If you turn the gas off, you will need a professional to turn it back on. Post a note telling others when you left and where you are going, and make arrangements for your pets.

Emergency Supplies Kit

Keep enough supplies in your home to last three days. Assemble a Disaster Supplies kit with items you may need in an evacuation. Store these supplies in sturdy, easy to carry containers, such as duffel bags or plastic totes.

- Water—a three-day supply of water (one gallon per person per day)

- Food—imperishable food

- One change of clothing and footwear per person

- One blanket and sleeping bag per person

- A first-aid kit that includes your family's prescription medications

- Emergency tools, including a battery powered radio, flashlight and plenty of extra batteries

- A set of car keys and credit card, cash or traveler's checks

- Sanitation supplies

- Special items for infants, elderly or disabled family members

- An extra pair of glasses

- Keep important family documents in a water-proof container

How to Have Positive Relationships

SECTION

5

How to Have Positive Relationshps

We have contacts with many people throughout our lives. Some persons we like, others we don't like. We especially like the people who make us feel good about ourselves. We value people we can trust. How do we find these people?

Write the names of people you know according to how close they are to you.

Self

Intimates

Friends

Acquaintances

Strangers

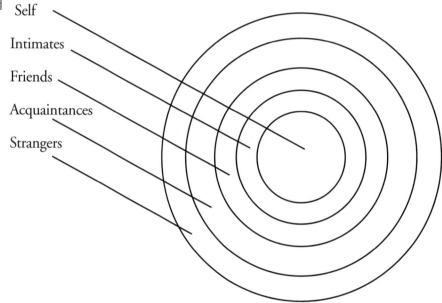

- Who would you trust with a secret?_____

- Who would never lie to you?_____

- Who will take care of you when you are ill?_____

- If you borrow money, whom will you pay back? _____

- Who makes you feel good about yourself? _____

- Who inspires you to do better? _____

Priorities

What is most important to you in your personal relations and life experiences?

Rate these items on a scale of 1 to 10. (ten being the highest value to you and one being the lowest or no value to you). Then share your results with someone and discuss why you are making this choice.

	Low value or no value 1	5	high value to me 10

1. Having a close-knit family...
2. Having a loving relationship ....
3. Being physically attractive ....
4. Having a comfortable marriage..
5. Getting two months vacation a year ....
6. Having a chance to be creative..
7. Making a difference in the world ....
8. Having freedom to make my own decisions ....
9. Having a beautiful home...
10. Having excellent health ....
11. Traveling around the world ....
12. Having honest friends ....
13. Having a sensuous sex life ....
14. Having a large personal library...
15. Having peace in the world ....
16. Being treated fairly ....
17. Having confidence in myself...
18. Having influence and power in my community ....
19. Having dependable transportation ....
20. Having someone who needs me...
21. Having someone to take care of me ....
22. Having not to worry about money ....
23. Having a gorgeous physical body ....
24. Having perfect children...
25. Being highly intelligent ....

Can you think of something that is important to you and is not listed here? Of those choices that you feel are most important to you, which one is absolutely number one in value to you? Why?

Personalities

Did you know that certain types of personalities tend to make certain choices in those things that they find most important? Do you know what personality type you are? You make choices according to whether you are an introvert or an extrovert, or whether you are more people oriented or thing oriented. Put an "x" on the line where you feel comfortable.

Extrovert_____Introvert
(outgoing and sociable)   (quiet and listening)

Now, put an "x" on the line where you feel more comfortable if you are more organized and detail oriented or more creative and disorganized.

Disorganized _____Organized
When the two lines above are crossed, the four personality quadrants are formed. Your personality will fall into the quadrant in which you feel most comfortable.

(Feeling)
Extrovert

Disorganized _____|_____ Organized
(Doing)   (Watching)

Introvert
(Thinking)

Each one of us falls into one of the above quadrants. We tend to get along better with people who are more like us, and we tend to have conflict with those who are opposite us. Do opposites attract? Why? What do you think? Does this make for a long-term commitment, or could it be short-lived? What would be best for you?

A   B   *FEELING*   C D

ENTHUSIASTIC

Gets involved with lots of new activities

A good starter

Gets other's opinions, feelings

Operates on trial and error "gut"

Needs to be with other people

Seeks out new experiences

Likes risks, excitement, change

Adapts to different situations well

Can be impulsive

Likes learning by doing

IMAGINATIVE

Sees lots of alternatives – whole picture

Uses imagination

Supportive to others – good listener

Creates with emotions

Needs some time alone

Uncomfortable with change

Observes others, asks questions

Likes assurance from others

Avoids conflict

Learns by listening

DOING   *WATCHING*

PRACTICAL

Applies ideas to solving problems

Has detective skills; searches and solves

Uses logic and reason to meet goals

Demands to be in control of situation

Sets up projects then delegates

Uses factual data, documented theories

Takes action on tasks, responsible

Wants results, no matter what

Can be impatient

Does not like emotions

LOGICAL

Likes theories – a good planner

Puts ideas together to make new

Very organized, precise, careful

Calculated all the possibilities

Works independently

Analyzes ideas, critical thinking

Avoids over involvement

Wants things done perfectly

Takes time to be correct

Unemotional

THINKING

1. How do others react to your personality?

2. What does your family think about you?

3. How about your boss?

4. What does your best friend think about you?

5. How do your children see you?

6. Is your personality different on the job? At home? With friends? How?

7. Have you ever been told that you are like – grandma? Your aunt? Another relative?

8. When you borrow something, do you return it? In good, or better, shape?

Items I need to Return

Item Borrowed	Lender	Date Borrowed	Date Returned	Condition

To be a good friend.

Abusive Relationships

When we choose persons for friendship or more intimate relationships, we make the best choices with the knowledge we have about them. Personality plays an important part, but so does that individual's values and priorities. Frequently, domestic violence becomes an issue because we have neglected our own values or beliefs.

Many women are interested in ways that they can predict whether they are about to become involved with someone who will be physically abusive. Below is a list of behaviors that are seen in males who beat their girlfriends or wives, or females who beat their husbands or lovers. The last four signs listed are almost always seen only if the person is a batterer. If the person has several of the other behaviors, say three or more, there is a strong potential for physical violence. The more signs the person has, the more likely the person is a batterer. In some cases, a batterer may have only a couple of behaviors that you can recognize, but they are very exaggerated, like extreme jealousy over ridiculous things. Initially, the batterer will try to explain his/her behavior as signs of his/her love and concern, and the partner may be flattered at first, but, as time goes on, the behaviors become more severe and serve to dominate the partner.

- **Jealousy:** At the beginning of a relationship, an abuser will always say that his jealousy is a sign of love. Jealousy has nothing to do with love. It's a sign of insecurity and possessiveness. He will question you about who you talk to, accuse you of flirting, or be jealous of times you spend with family, friends, or children. As the jealousy progresses, he may call you frequently during the day or drop by unexpectedly. He may refuse to let you work for fear you will meet someone else, or even do strange behaviors such as checking your car mileage or asking friends to spy on you.

- **Controlling Behavior:** At first the batterer will say that this behavior is because he's concerned for your safety, your need to use your time well, or your need to make good decisions. He will be angry if you are "late" coming back from the store or an appointment. He will question you closely about where you went, who you talked to. As this behavior gets worse, he may not let you make personal decisions about the house, your clothing, going to church. He may keep all the money or even make you ask permission to leave the house or room.

- **Quick Involvement:** Many battered women dated or knew their abuser for less than six months before they were engaged or living together. He comes on like a whirlwind, "You are the only person I could ever talk to…", "I've never felt loved like this by anyone…" He needs someone desperately and will pressure you to commit to him.

- **Unrealistic Expectations:** He is very dependent on you for all of his needs. He expects you to be the perfect wife, mother, lover, friend. He will say things like, "If you loved me…." "I'm all you need—you are all I need…" You are supposed to take care of everything for him emotionally and in the home.

- **Isolation:** The man tries to cut you off from all resources. If you have men friends, you are a "whore". If you have women friends, you are a "lesbian". If you are close to family, you are "tied to the apron strings…". He accuses people who are your supports of "causing trouble". He may want to live in the country without a phone. He may not let you use the car, or he may try to keep you from working or going to school.

- **Blames Others for His Problems:** If he is chronically unemployed, someone is always doing him wrong, or out to "get" him. He may make mistakes and then blame you for upsetting him and keeping him from concentrating on doing his job. He will tell you that you are at fault for almost anything that goes wrong.

- **Blames Others for His Feelings:** He will tell you, "You make me mad!" "You are hurting me by not doing what I ask!" "I can't help being angry!" "You control how I feel!" He really makes the decision about what he thinks and feels, but will use the feelings to manipulate you. Harder to catch are his claims that ,"You make me happy!"

- **Hypersensitivity:** The man is easily insulted, he claims his feelings are "hurt" when he's really very mad, or he takes the slightest setback as a personal attack. He will rant and rave about the injustice of things that have happened to him, things that are really just part of living, like being asked to work over-time, getting a traffic ticket, being told that something he does is annoying, being asked to help with chores.

- **Cruelty to Animals or Children:** This is a man who punishes animals brutally or is insensitive to their pain or suffering. He may expect children to be capable of doing things far beyond their ability (i.e. whips a 2-year-old for wetting diaper) or he may tease children or young brothers and sisters until they cry. 60% of men who beat the women they are with also beat their children. He may not want children to eat at the table or expect them to keep to their room all evening while he is home.

- **"Playful" Use of Force in Sex:** This man may like to throw you down and hold you down during sex. He may want to act out fantasies during sex, where you are helpless. He is letting you know that the idea of "rape" excites him. He may show little concern about whether you want to have sex and use sulking or anger to manipulate you into compliance. He may start having sex with you while you are sleeping, or demand sex when you are ill or tired.

- **Verbal Abuse:** In addition to saying things that are meant to be cruel and hurtful, this can be seen by the man degrading you, cursing you, running down any of your accomplishments. The man will tell you that you are stupid and unable to function without him. This may involve waking you to verbally abuse you or not letting you sleep.

- **Rigid Sex Roles:** The man expects you to serve him. He will say you must stay at home, that you must obey him in all things – even things that are criminal in nature. The abuser will see all women as inferior to men, more stupid, unable to be a whole person without a relationship.

- **Dr. Jekyll and Mr. Hyde:** Many women are confused by their abuser's "sudden" changes in mood. They will describe that one minute he's nice and the next minute he explodes, some special "mental problem" or that he is "crazy". Explosiveness and mood swings are typical of men who beat their partners, and these behaviors are related to other characteristics such as hypersensitivity.

- **Past Battering:** The man may say he has hit women in the past, but they made him do it. You may hear from the relatives or ex-spouses that the man is abusive. A batterer will beat any woman he is with. Situational circumstances do not make a person an abusive personality.

- **Threats of Violence:** This would include any threat of physical force meant to control you: "I'll slap your mouth off!" "I'll kill you!" "I'll break your neck!" Most men do not threaten their mates, but a batterer will try to excuse this behavior by saying, "Everybody talks like that!" He also chooses friends who talk like that, with the same attitude.

- **Breaking or Striking Objects:** This behavior is used as a punishment (breaking loved ones possessions), but is mostly used to terrorize you into submission. The man may beat on tables with his fist or throw objects around or near you. Again, this is a very remarkable behavior. Only very immature people beat on objects in the presence of other people in order to threaten them.

- **Any Force During an Argument:** This may involve a man holding you down, physically restraining you from leaving the room, any pushing or shoving. The man may hold you against a wall and say, "Now you are going to listen to me!" His brute strength is used against you and is an unfair advantage.

Questions to think about

Has your partner/spouse ever…

- ☐ said he would physically hurt the children if you left?
- ☐ said he would take the children away and not let you see them?
- ☐ told the children that you are to blame for all the problems?
- ☐ threatened to get legal custody of the children away from you?
- ☐ not paid child support?
- ☐ told you that you would be out on the street if you left?
- ☐ bought the children gifts, toys, etc., to be the "good" guy?
- ☐ threatened that they will retaliate if you don't do what they want you to do?
- ☐ made threats that would harm family members?
- ☐ threatened to hurt or kill family pets?
- ☐ threatened to destroy possessions or other household things?

- ☐ happen to "just lose" your things?
- ☐ tell you that no one would ever believe you if you told what was going on?
- ☐ threaten that Child Protective Services will come and take the kids?
- ☐ insisted that you only go to his/her family at holidays?
- ☐ tried to turn the kids against you or other members of your family?
- ☐ exaggerated any small mistake you make, and made an issue of it?
- ☐ taken advantage of any past mistakes you have made?
- ☐ embarrassed you in public or made demeaning remarks to you?
- ☐ coerced you by threatening or physical acts, holding you back, grabbing you?
- ☐ forced you to look at them when they talk to you?
- ☐ pushed or shoved you around?
- ☐ grabbed the baby away from you?
- ☐ battered you by hitting, slapping, kicking, biting, pinching, scratching, choking, pulling hair, and breaking teeth?
- ☐ stabbed you with a knife or shot you with a gun?
- ☐ cut your hair, or threatened to disfigure you in some way?
- ☐ burned you with cigarettes, lighters, or matches?
- ☐ rammed you with the car?
- ☐ shattered the windshield of the car you were in while in a rage?
- ☐ broke furniture or destroyed doors and windows in the house?
- ☐ slashed the car tires so you could not leave, or do other damage to the car?
- ☐ told you to lie about injuries that you have received, or refused to let you get treatment for injuries received?
- ☐ withheld affection as a means to punish you?
- ☐ belittle you or tell you that you are stupid, incompetent, and foolish?
- ☐ not allow you to visit your friends and family?
- ☐ made it too difficult for you to go to work?
- ☐ told you that you could not go to work outside the home?
- ☐ refused to give you money for purchases you needed to make?
- ☐ lied about money or destroyed bills so you wouldn't see them?
- ☐ insisted on always being with you to get groceries, go to doctor's office or other appointments?
- ☐ insisted on the control of all the money, checkbook, and checks?
- ☐ wanted you to live in isolated housing?
- ☐ not allowed you to drive or have access to a car?
- ☐ taken the phone away from you and/or forbidden you to use it?
- ☐ refuse to perform parenting responsibility when it is their turn?
- ☐ made a public display of sexualized behavior towards you like patting your behind, pinching your breasts, grabbing your privates?
- ☐ promise you favors, gifts, or privileges for performing certain sex acts?
- ☐ photographed you during sexual activity?
- ☐ raped you and stated that it was OK to do in your relationship?

- ☐ caused physical injury due to aggressive sexual activity?
- ☐ demand to be treated as "King of the Castle"?
- ☐ gone out for a night "with the boys/girls" but refuses to let you do the same?

Have you ever said:

- ☐ he/she didn't mean to do it?
- ☐ it's not his/her fault, it is mine because I am so stupid?
- ☐ he/she didn't do it?
- ☐ he/she was under a lot of stress?
- ☐ he/she was drunk and couldn't be held accountable?
- ☐ the kids didn't behave, or I could not control them, and it made him/her angry?
- ☐ I did not fix what he/she wanted for dinner?
- ☐ I know he/she will never do it again?
- ☐ He/she was just mad because my mom/sister/friend came over and I didn't get the housecleaning done?
- ☐ I need to be perfect so he/she won't get angry with me?
- ☐ It is all my fault?

It is difficult to get out of an abusive relationship if you are co-dependent. However, children are greatly affected by abuse between the adults in their lives. You may need to really think how your actions are affecting your children, as well as yourself, if you are in an abusive relationship.

Power and Control in Dating

Look For:

Physical Abuse: Any attempt to hurt or scare partner physically. Hitting, biting, hair pulling, grabbing, pushing, shoving, tripping, kicking.

Verbal Abuse: Name Calling, embarrassments, criticizing, publicly humiliating, put downs.

Psychological and Emotional Abuse: Putting your partner down and making them feel bad about themselves. Mind games or making partner feel crazy. Telling "secrets" to others. Ignoring or giving the "silent treatment".

Destruction of Personal Property: Destroying personal effects (pictures, letters, clothing, gifts.) Ruining belongings. Defacing or causing damage to partner's home or auto.

Threats, Anger, and Intimidation: Using looks, actions, expressions or a loud voice to intimidate partner. Smashing or throwing objects. Threatening to leave partner or abandoning him or her in a dangerous place. Threatening physical harm.

Jealousy, Isolation, Possessiveness, and Restriction of Freedoms: Using jealousy as a sign of love instead of insecurity. Controlling what partner does, whom partner sees and talks to, where partner goes. Refusing to let partner work or join activities. Dropping by unexpectedly to "watch" activities. Accusations of cheating on partner.

Sexual Abuse: Unwanted or uncomfortable touching. Continued sexual advances after being told "no". Forced sex. "Playful" use of force during sex. Treating partner like a sex object.

Abuse of "Privilege": Making all the decisions. Going out with the "girls" or the "boys", but not allowing partner that freedom. Walking out on an argument and leaving partner. Doing all the telephoning and expecting partner to be there.

Any of the above behaviors are not mature or healthy to engage in!

Let's Talk Abut Sex

Sex involves a relationship with another person. Sex can be meaningful or meaningless, it all depends on what you want in your life. If you choose to have sexual relationships without a commitment or value, you open yourself up to disease and disappointment. You must get real about sex in your life. A great deal of our self-esteem comes from the knowledge that our parents loved and respected one another. Children should not be gotten through meaningless sexual encounters. You must get to know your partner well before intimacy begins. If you wish to have a meaningful sexual relationship, then you need to be certain that your partner has similar values and beliefs as you do. This means you will need to discuss sex and sexual issues with your partner, before you have the first sexual encounter! Here are some questions that can help you talk about sex.

Agree or Disagree: tell why you make this choice

1. Women work just as hard as men.

2. The husband should be willing to move if the wife's job demands it.

3. Women should be able to have abortion on demand.

4. Women are instinctively maternal and nurturing.

5. Women should be free to pursue many areas of employment because modern men need women who are interesting, flexible, and capable.

6. Sex roles are obsolete, and we should move toward a culture in which there are not "female" or "male" roles.

7. Women can and should try to be like men.

8. Men and women have the same biological range of emotion and intellectual capabilities. The differences present in our society are all learned.

9. Women can best overcome discrimination by working in all women groups, or classes.

10. Almost all men are sexists, either consciously or unconsciously.

11. The husband should have the final decision on all important matters.

12. A sexual act should bring an increased capacity to trust self and others.

13. A sexual act should increase the possibility of honesty and openness.

14. A sexual act should allow complete freedom for the individual.

15. A sexual act should allow people to "do their own thing"

16. A sexual act between persons of the same sex is OK.

17. Saying "no" to sex is respected.

Which opinion is true for you?

1. In a sexual relationship, I would prefer that:

    a. Sex be more meaningful to me than to the other person.

    b. Sex be more meaningful to the other person than to me.

    c. Sex be meaningful to neither one of us.

2. The worst thing that I could find out about my partner, husband or wife, is that he/she:

    a. Has AIDS

    b. Is sterile

    c. Sleeps with anybody

Rules for Fair Fighting

Instructions: Keeping in mind your most recent disagreement, read through the following rules for fair fighting. Place an X before each rule that you think you might have violated in the course of the argument and place an O before each rule that you thought your opponent violated. When you are both finished with this, exchange papers and discuss the rules for fair fighting that you want to work on for the interests of your family.

YOU   OPPONENT

☐ 1. ***Fight by mutual consent:*** Don't insist on a fight at a time when one of you can't ☐
handle this type of strain. A good fight demands two ready participants.

☐ 2. ***Stick to the present:*** Don't dredge up past mistakes and faults about which you ☐
can do nothing

☐ 3. ***Stick to the subject:*** Limit this fight to this subject. Don't throw every other ☐
problem into it—take them at a different time.

☐ 4. ***Don't hit below the belt:*** Don't throw sensitive areas at each other. ☐

☐ 5. ***Don't quit! Work it out:*** Bring the fight to a mutual conclusion, so it will ☐
not recur again and again.

☐ 6. ***Don't try to win, EVER:*** If one wins, the other loses and begins to build ☐
resentment about this relationship.

☐ 7. ***Respect crying:*** It is a valid response to how we feel, but don't let tears ☐
sidetrack you.

☐ 8. ***Hold Hands:*** Touching another most often softens our words and makes ☐
us more unwilling to hurt the other.

☐ 9. ***NO VIOLENCE:*** Physical violence negates all the above rules for fair ☐
fighting.

REMEMBER: A fight between family members has the purpose of clearing the air and expressing deep feelings in order to build a more unified life. Keep your goal in mind – the goal of sharing your lives with each other and to provide a good role model for your children.

Personal Boundaries

How I treat you

How I let you treat me

What are boundaries?

A boundary is a limit that defines where one thing ends and another begins. There are all kinds of boundaries. They teach us responsibility in all areas of our life. We violate boundaries when we fail to do the things we are supposed to do or do things we are NOT supposed to do, and allow other people to make us do things that we should not do.

Physical Boundaries:

The world has many countries. Each country has boundaries that show where it begins and ends. These countries are different for the people living there – in the language they speak, the food they eat and the clothes they wear. There are cities and villages and towns in each country existing in definite places. If we want to go to Boston, we know where to find it. It will be in a certain place on the earth. In the cities, people live in houses. The houses have an address where you can find them. People live in dwellings that have walls and roofs and keep the rain and storms out. Each dwelling has specific doors and windows where the people can come and go or look through. There are property boundaries, and some people put up fences to show where the line is.

Our skin is a boundary for our bodies. It holds us together and keeps our insides from falling out. It protects us by letting us know when we are too hot or too cold, or when we are uncomfortable. But, it too can be violated. When it is cut or injured, it is painful and can let harmful germs enter our body, which can make us sick or even kill us. When we are sick, we cannot do our best. We cannot work or play or live.

People Boundaries:

When two or more people come together, they can choose to interact with each other, or they can go their separate ways. When people choose to relate, there are behaviors that are appropriate, which tell us that these people are safe to let into our lives. Some people are strangers that we nod and smile at, but never know their names or anything about them. That is a distant boundary, or far away from us. Other people we think of as friends. They are closer to us. Some friends we can see occasionally and other friends are even closer. We like to see them often and talk to them. Then there are those persons who we let into our lives and into our homes. They can be a friend as well as a lover. We can trust them. We feel safe with them. We tell them our secrets and dreams. We also need to understand our own inner boundaries. If we are not in touch with ourselves and we do not understand our own feelings, thoughts, and hopes, we can be violated easily. When we have a violation in our relationship, it is painful and can make us sick, too. How can we tell what appropriate boundaries are when we relate to other people?

Spiritual Boundaries:

When we have healthy spiritual boundaries, we have the ability to discover what is and what is not the truth. The human spirit can be very strong and can heal the most devastating pain, unless it has been violated. The abuse which is caused by someone in authority or who has power over us causes our spirit to break. The rules that are enforced by fear, guilt and shame are usually unwritten and unspoken, but they are an attempt to maintain control over us. It is rebellious to disagree. When an institution states that you must join because they are the "best" or the "only" or condemn you for not belonging, it has become a false god. This is a spiritual violation and robs a real relationship with God. Each person can find the grace and redemption through finding God for himself or herself for a personal relationship.

Sexual Boundaries:

Healthy sexual boundaries give us a positive sense of ourselves as male or female. It helps us discern what is appropriate dress and what is inappropriate. It helps us choose who can touch us and where we can be touched. It provides guidance for what is positive and makes us feel whole about ourselves. We can determine what is pornography and what is art to us. Sex is the most intimate and vulnerable part of our lives and can help fulfill our self-esteem or destroy it with boundary violation.

Emotional Boundaries:

These boundaries determine how we let other people treat us. They set limits on what is safe and appropriate for us to feel. When we have a healthy self-image, we have healthy relationships and can take others into our lives to share happiness and growth in life.

If we do not know our own feelings about something, we can never have an intimate relationship with another person because they will not know how we feel about something either. Boundaries are unhealthy and dysfunctional when they are too close or too distant, too rigid or too flexible, too loose or too tight.

Questions to help you find your own boundaries

1. How do you define your "space"

2. Do you have time for yourself? What do you do when someone else demands your time?

3. List your friends and place them as how close or distant you see them to you.

4. List acquaintances, people you know, but not well. Are there any who you would like to have closer to you?

5. After you have mapped out friends and acquaintances, put in your family members.

6. What can you do to not allow yourself to be manipulated by another person?

7. Are you being physically abused in your life now?

8. What do you need to do to protect yourself from physical abuse?

9. Do you often put yourself down and feel bad?

10. Do you lie about yourself to make yourself look good?

11. Do you have violent outbursts of temper?

12. Do you apologize even when it is not your fault?

13. Do you call someone else ugly and hurtful names?

14. Are you being mentally or emotionally abusive to another person now?

15. Do you look to other people to take care of you and your problems?

16. Do you hide your needs from others?

17. If you are in an abusive relationship, where did you find the person that you chose to come into your life? What attracted you to this person?

18. Can you trust your brothers and/or sisters? Why? If not, why not?

19. Did your parents respect and support each other?

20. Do you and your partner respect and support each other?

21. Do you respect and support your child (ren)?

22. How have you been emotionally violated by someone who was too intrusive?

23. How have you been emotionally intrusive and to whom?

24. Would you feel comfortable going into someone else's home when no one was home?

25. Who would you allow to come into your home when you are not there?

26. Would you go through someone's pockets or purse without their knowledge?

27. When would you allow someone to go through your wallet or purse without your knowledge?

28. How do you feel about graffiti? Have you ever written or made marks on public property?

29. Has anyone ever marked up something you own?

30. Have you ever had someone come and take away a friend from you? What did they do and how did they do it? How did you feel about it?

31. What should happen to a person who steals?

32. Is telling a lie a boundary violation? To whom?

33. When you are talking to someone and another person butts into your conversation, how do you feel? Is this a violation?

34. What about secrets? When are they good? When are they harmful?

35. How do you feel if someone listens in on your conversations?

36. Should parents feel that it is Ok to read a child's diary without their knowledge?

37. Have you ever had someone spread a rumor about you? How did you feel?

38. When someone makes a promise to you and they don't keep it, how do you feel?

39. Do you make promises you don't intend to keep?

40. When someone says they love you, but violate your boundaries, do you feel like they really do love you?

41. How do you build trust with someone?

42. How can you get someone else to trust you?

We put people in jail who violate other person's boundaries, which is a way of making them recognize boundaries. Are there other ways we can teach others about appropriate boundaries?

If someone is violating your boundaries, make a plan on how to regain your respect and dignity and write it down here. It will be easier to follow through on this plan when you need it.

_____

_____

_____

_____

_____

_____

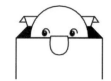

Understanding Sexual Abuse

The whole topic of sexuality has long been confusing and secretive simply because it has not been a topic open for discussion. Why not? It certainly plays a major role in the life of every individual. It would seem that, something this important should be a positively embracing, warmly affirming, communication between individuals who strongly care for each other. Using positive sexual contact can confirm trust and the nurture of belonging. Love regenerates enthusiasm and productivity. However, any abuse of a sexual nature destroys personhood.

Sexual abuse is the unequal strength of one person attempting to find self-gratification or excitement at the expense of another individual.

1). It can be physical. This is a hands on, touching in a sexual way, rubbing, fondling, stroking, including oral and anal sex, masturbation, and intercourse. It does not make a difference whether or not the victim is clothed, as the intent of the abuse is the same. The feelings of the victim are not considered. Although the physical abuse can be a violent attack, it more frequently occurs as a coercion by a person who another individual likes, trusts and wants to please. There may be rewards given, such as money or emotional rewards such as sharing a "secret". However, they are often threatened with violence or withdrawal of love if they tell anyone else about it. Thus, some victims feel they are to blame for the abuse.

2). Overt sexual abuse is the sexual stimulation received by one person, through voyeurism or exhibitionism, whether done to another or forcing another to do it at their expense. This kind of abuse can be conscious, where the abuser is stimulated by watching an unknowing person undress, or it can also be an unconscious sexual stimulation where excitement is generated by titillation of an inappropriate or unwilling person. Pornography is sexual abuse. Again, this sexual abuse concerns the stimulation of one person at another individual's embarrassment or expense.

3). Covert sexual abuse involves:
     a. Inappropriate sexual talking, where dirty sexual jokes are told for another's embarrassment, or persons are called by obscene and sexual names such as slut, dick-head, boobs, or homo, or sexual remarks are made to degrade another's body or body parts. Obscene phone calls are sexually abusive. What is sexual harassment? Sexual harassment are offenses, whether intentional or not, that can be jokes or comments about sex or explicit invitations to have sex. Displaying sexually suggestive objects, photos or cartoons. Remarks about a person's body or sexual attractiveness. Whistling, gawking or commenting on body parts, pro or con. Touching, leering, whistling or making insulting, suggestive or obscene comments or gestures. Sexual harassment has become such a concern in the workplace that it could result in dismissal because it reduces work productivity. This also includes the lack of parental responsibility in teaching their children about adequate sexual information. The streets are not the place to learn how to love and care for each other. That is what families are for.

     b. Boundary violations where appropriate regard for another's space and privacy are ignored: Walking in when another person is in the bathroom without permission. Children witnessing their parents in sexual behavior. Parents need to model appropriate respect and dignity and set appropriate sexual boundaries. Nudity is not sexual abuse, but it is dysfunctional in our society when displayed inappropriately.

4). Emotional sexual abuse results when parents romanticize and sexualize their relationship with their children, such as "Daddy's little princess" or "Mamma's little Man". Here, the child is expected to take care of the parent's needs and is, in fact, abandoned to his own needs. This emotional abuse can also be found where one parent contaminates the child's feeling about the other parent and all others in the same vein: "All men are sex fiends" or "All women are seductresses". When one feels only valued because of their gender and sexualized body parts, like big boobs or big biceps, it can overwhelm the real person inside. An unfortunate accident can destroy a person who has nothing to fall back on. Beauty fades, but the authentic person can be strong for a full lifetime.

There is a great emphasis on sex in our society, specifically in advertising, where sex is used to sell cars to ice cream. It is important for parents to point out the fallacy between the media hype and real life. The sexual curiosity is diverted by MTV and other lurid songs from a search for friendship and positive human relationships. It is important to find real live persons to care about and share our lives with, and commit to positive relationships. Sex with many persons is empty intimacy and can pose a serious health risk. No one should feel pressured into having sex. Prostitutes who have sex for a living state that they do not enjoy sex because it is no longer a special bonding for them. It is much more fulfilling to wait on sexual activity until you can make mature choices for yourself, and these choices also include supporting yourself and taking responsibility for yourself. Then, when you choose to have children, they will grow up knowing their parents loved, respected and cared for each other.

What is Criminal Sexual Conduct?

The following personal injury/victim incapacity definitions for various criminal sexual conduct charges are:

1st Degree CSC: includes penetration plus any one of the following:
        victim under the age of 13
        victim 13-15/blood affinity
        victim 13-15 position of authority
        felony, multiple actors/force
        multiple actors/victim incapacity
        weapon
        personal injury/force
Penalty: Any number of years up to life in prison.

2nd Degree CSC: Includes contact plus any one of the circumstances listed above.
Penalty: up to 15 years in prison.

3rd Degree CSC: Includes penetration plus any of the following:
        victim 13-15,
        victim incapacitated
        force or coercion (threats, extortion, medical treatment, element of surprise).
Penalty: up to 15 years in prison.

4th Degree CSC: Includes contact plus either incapacitated victim force or coercion (but without element of surprise).
Penalty: Prison

Parenting

SECTION
6

Children's Rights

1. **Physical Needs**
The physical needs of children are vital to develop healthy bodies and good health habits. Accidents and illness that can be prevented are necessary to reduce medical costs. The essential needs of children are nutritious and safe food, adequate sleep, suitable clothing for the weather, a safe and sanitary living environment, medical and dental care when needed, and guidance in good health practices, such as immunizations, physical education and safety and security.

2. **Emotional Needs**
These needs include stability in the home, familiarity with adult caregivers, a sense of belonging, a feeling of being wanted by the group, a feeling of being able to contribute to that group with high self-esteem, intellectual training in the ability to think clearly and to solve problems wisely and without violence. There is a need for social approval and for the encouragement in achievement with satisfaction in making things and doing jobs with a view towards vocational guidance, self-support, and a share in the community. There is also a need for independence and guidance in self-control and self-direction. Family communication is the foundation for meeting many of these needs.

3. **Spiritual Needs**
These needs include compassion and emotional intelligence. It suggests the value of the individual and positive, supportive relationships to others. It teaches the appropriate aspects of friendship and love without exploitation. It sets the values of living, which make goal setting attainable and a feeling of self-worth.

4. **Mental Needs**
These needs include access to education, access to mentoring, and access to resources to answer questions, encouragement for achievement and acknowledgement for attempts. Healthy mental health is a feeling of self-control, self-worth, and the ability to make the lives of others in the community better.

Children need to be protected and guided as they are not able to provide for their own needs for quite a few years. When adults conceive a child, they must be able and willing to provide for that child's needs. It is the parents responsibility to see that the child's needs are met.

A parent's responsibility is to raise their children to be adults.

What are the "adult life roles" that you think your children should be able to take as they reach adulthood?

1. They should have motivation to achieve a goal.
2. They should enjoy reading for their own pleasure.
3. They should participate in school.
4. They should realize their responsibility in doing their own homework.
5. They should be proud of their school.
6. They should have concern for equality and social justice.
7. They should have integrity.
8. They should value honesty.
19. They should be able to demonstrate restraint.
10. They should be able to plan and make decisions.
11. They should be able to make friends and cooperate with others.
12. They should show tolerance for other cultures.
13. They should be able to resist peer pressure when it could be detrimental.
14. They should be able to peacefully resolve conflicts.
15. They should have a sense of personal power through self-esteem and confidence.
16. They should have a positive view of their own future.

These good qualities are developed by:

1. Positive family support.
2. Time at home with family members.
3. Positive family communication.
4. Living in a caring neighborhood.
5. Having other positive adult relationships.
6. Having a caring school climate.
7. Parent involvement and interest in schooling.
8. Safety in the home, neighborhood, and community.
9. Positive adult role models.
10. Positive peer influence.
11. Encouragement to provide service to others.
12. Belonging to a religious community to learn values.
13. Encouragement to have creative hobbies and activities.
14. Understanding and support of family boundaries.
15. Understanding and support of school boundaries.
16. Understanding and support of community boundaries.
17. High expectations to fulfill their potential.

What are you doing to help your child?

What would you do differently from your parents?

As a child, you grew up with parents who did the best they knew how to do. What do you wish your parents would have learned to help you be the best person you could be? How do you feel your parents made an impact on your life—for good, or for bad. Do you wish your parents had spent more time with you? Did they talk to you enough? Do you think they understood you fully? What would you like to have done with your parents that you did not do? If there was conflict, how did it work out? As an adult, will you be friends with your parents? Do you want your parents to remain a part of your life? What do you think a good parent is like? Write your comments here.

_____

_____

_____

_____

_____

_____

_____

_____

_____

_____

_____

_____

_____

_____

_____

_____

Parent Assessment

This assessment gives you an idea of what parental behavior is regarded in child abuse and neglect cases. Judge for yourself.

Parenting Skills	LOW			HIGH
1. Parents show they can provide emotional stability, sense of values, and physical nurturance to child	1	2	3	4
2. Parents know what is appropriate for the age and ability of child and sees that their child gets adequate rest at night	1	2	3	4
3. Parents show that they can provide consistent and reasonable punishment and rewards for child's behavior that is not hurtful nor harmful	1	2	3	4
4. Parents always have adequate supervision of child in any environment	1	2	3	4
5. Parents understand the importance that children go to school regularly with good attendance	1	2	3	4
6. Parents show that they keep a standard of health care, dress and personal hygiene that is healthy for their family	1	2	3	4

Sense of Community				
7. The family has frequent contact with friends and/or relatives and other informal support systems in enjoyable company	1	2	3	4
8. The family seeks informal support systems for advice and help	1	2	3	4
9. The family knows about and uses those professional or community resources when needed for the health and happiness of the family	1	2	3	4
10. Parents enjoy leisure and recreational activities and get time for their own activities for health and happiness	1	2	3	4
11. The family has remained in same dwelling for several months and does not have a pattern of frequent moves	1	2	3	4
12. The parents are able to be employed at this time	1	2	3	4
13. The parents maintain a satisfactory work record	1	2	3	4
14. The parents show physical and/or verbal affection towards all family members on a daily basis	1	2	3	4
15. The parents have developed cooperation and members share responsibilities and talk out differences.	1	2	3	4
16. The family enjoys doing activities together	1	2	3	4

	LOW			HIGH
17. There is not a lot of fighting in the family. Conflicts are talked out	1	2	3	4
18. Parents have discussed and come to agreement about important things and discipline, working together on critical issues and discipline.	1	2	3	4
19. Spouses or other primary caretakers share common interests and activities	1	2	3	4

Impulse Control

	LOW			HIGH
20. Parents do not lose emotional control and can cope with crisis when necessary	1	2	3	4
21. Parents have self-discipline and can control their anger	1	2	3	4
22. Parents show that they can delay gratification of their own wishes for the best interests of their child	1	2	3	4
23. Parents do not have problems with drug and/or alcohol usage	1	2	3	4
24. Parents work together to budget money and manage resources	1	2	3	4

Self-Esteem

25. Parents understand the limits of their own skills and abilities	1	2	3	4
26. Parents show adequate personal hygiene and appearance	1	2	3	4
27. Parents are interested in their own good health and fitness	1	2	3	4
28. Parents show capacity to trust others when it is appropriate	1	2	3	4
29. Parents show maturity or judgment when making decisions	1	2	3	4
30. Parents make sincere and strong efforts at resolving any child protection regarding abuse and neglect	1	2	3	4

In your opinion, is parent of child likely to show neglect or abuse pattern?   Yes   No

Parenting is a difficult job. No child comes with a book of instructions, which would make it much easier. However, if you need help, taking classes and workshops, reading books and magazines, or getting advice from family and friends, don't be afraid to ask for it. You and your child will benefit.

During your child's infancy, you are mainly a caregiver. You must meet your child's needs for feeding, changing, cleaning, dressing and loving.

As your child grows, you become a teacher, to explain about all the joys and wonders of the world. You will explain why things happen and how things work. Your child will have many questions, if you are doing your job correctly. You will also be a counselor, guiding your child through bad times by giving love, support and direction. Every child is different and has unique needs. Seek expert help if you need it.

The Parent is the Child's Teacher

Your child has five senses: Touch, Taste, Sight, Smell and Hearing. Playing games with your child in each of these areas is fun for both of you. You may think up games of your own, but here are a few ideas to get you started:

1. **Touch:** We tell how rough or smooth things are, or how hot or cold, or how heavy or light. Put items under a blanket or in a bag, like a clothespin, small toy, or plastic animal. Start with only 3 objects. Ask your child to give you one of the items, say the clothespin. You can also have a matching item in your hand. Have your child feel for the clothespin to find it. As your child gets older, he/she might be comfortable wearing an eye mask to not see and play the game. If you were blind, you can tell what things are by feeling them. Children like to play this game. Can you tell what the temperature is, just by holding out your hand?

2. You can write letters and numbers on your child's back with your finger. See if he/she can guess what you have written. Try other areas of the body, like the back of the hand or top of the foot. Give each other messages without talking!

3. **Taste:** Play guessing games of what does this taste like? Mashed vegetables are fun, as only the color gives a clue. Use food coloring to change the clues to the food. Use a blindfold to taste different foods. Identify different nuts, like peanuts, almonds, pecans, walnuts, cashews and brazil nuts.

4. **Smell:** We can tell a lot about our surroundings by what we smell. Put drops of different flavorings on cotton balls, mix them up and see if your child can match the smells. Use good smells and bad ones, like orange, cherry, lemon, peanut butter and garlic. Smell different flowers in the garden with your eyes closed and see if you can tell what flower you are smelling.

5. **Sight:** There is so much to see. We see color, light, depth, etc. Encourage your child to draw what he sees and you will guess what that is. It's a game of "I Spy". Find some small color paint patches at the hardware store and cut them in two to make matching colors. Mix them in a box and see if your child can match the color. Play a card game with these patches. The one with the most color matches wins.

6. **Hearing:** We can teach our hearing to have a perfect pitch. Listen to sounds. Try to identify what they are. Listen to sounds very far away. You can hear snow falling if you are quiet. Use a musical instrument to get different pitches. Try to match the pitch with singing.

You should read to your child every day. Read books chapter by chapter, and every time you stop between chapters, ask you child what he/she thinks is going to happen in the story. Make up your own stories, or tell stories about you and your family. What is your favorite story?

The best part of having a child is to be a child again yourself. Whether you enjoyed your own childhood or not, you get a chance to see what fun can be with your child. Every day can be a beautiful day to play!

Possible Symptoms in Children Who Witness Adult Abuse

- Sleeplessness, fear of going to sleep, nightmares, dreams of danger

- Headaches, stomachaches

- Anxiety about being hurt or killed, hyper vigilance about danger

- Fighting with others, hurting other children or animals

- Temper tantrums

- Withdrawal from other people and activities

- Listlessness, depression, little energy for life

- Feelings of loneliness and isolation

- Substance abuse

- Suicide attempts or engaging in dangerous behavior

- Fear of going to school or of separating from mother, truancy

- Stealing

- Frozen watchfulness or excessive fear

- Acting perfect, overachieving, behaving like small adults

- Worrying, difficulties in concentrating and paying attention

- Bed-wetting or regression to earlier developmental stages

- Eating problems

- Medical problems like asthma, arthritis, ulcers

- Denial of any problem or dissociation

- Identification with the aggressor

- Over controlling behavior with siblings

Pre-Kindergarten Assessment

This assessment will give you an idea of what skills your child needs to enter kindergarten. You are your child's first teacher and will need to teach and reinforce these skills, even if you have used pre-school or daycare.

1. Can count by rote to _____.
2. Can recite the alphabet.
3. Matches quantity to symbol, 1 through 10.
4. Has basic time skills (can identify the numbers and the hands of the clock and the direction the hands turn).
5. Can recognize money (and give the value and name of penny, nickel, dime, quarter).
6. Writes numbers sequentially to _____.
7. Recognizes numerals to _____.
8. Can tell ordinal position (first, last, second, middle, third, fourth, fifth).
9. Prints lower case letters, as dictated.
10. Prints upper case letters, as dictated.
11. Prints lower case letters sequentially (abcdef).
12. Prints upper case letters sequentially. (ABCDEF).
13. Names upper case letters.
14. Matches lower case letters.
15. Answers "Where do we go when we….?" (need a haircut, are sick, etc.)
16. Answers "Why do we have people?" (Doctors, nurses, teachers, firemen, etc.)
17. Answers "Why do we have objects?" (beds, stoves, keys, locks, etc.)
18. Answers "What do you do when you…?" (you want a drink, cut your finger, see your shoe is untied, see a house on fire…etc.)
19. Classifying (can name what makes a group of unlike objects similar: a ball, wagon, jump rope and doll would be toys).
20. Weather (can name various pictures of weather as "rainy" ,"cold", "cloudy", etc.
21. Directions/positional concepts (up/down, forward/backward, in/out, etc.)
22. Quantitative concepts (more/less, many/few, thick/thin, etc.)
23. Names basic shapes (circle, square, triangle, rectangle, diamond).
24. Knows right and left.
25. Can match, identify and name colors: pink, gray, white, purple, brown and black.
26. Can match, identify and name orange, red, blue, green and yellow.
27. Shows and names parts of the body: heel, elbow, ankle, shoulder, jaw, wrist, waist and chin.
28. Knows beside, below, above, under, behind, and in front.
29. Knows telephone number.
30. Knows birthday (month and date).
31. Knows what town he/she lives in.
32. Repeats series of unrelated numbers (5-8-3-5, 2-9-4-1, etc.)
33. Buttons clothes.
34. Snaps clothes.
35. Zips own coat.
36. Ties own shoes.
37. Cuts on lines, curved and straight.
38. Holds scissors correctly and moves paper when cutting.
39. Copies a square, triangle, rectangle and +.
40. Copies a circle, horizontal line, vertical line and a V.
41. Prints first name.
42. Traces letters.
43. Holds pencil correctly. 3 fingers/2 fingers.
44. Makes a line with a ruler.
45. Laces a "sewing board".
46. Folds and creases paper.
47. Catches a ball with hands only.
48. Walks forward and backward with balance on a 3-inch wide balance beam.
49. Hops repeatedly with balance on the right and left foot.
50. Jumps at least four inches off floor repeatedly with balance.

How to Measure for Children's Clothes

Check for a good fit:

Buy by child's size not age.

Can child sit, stoop and stretch without clothes binding?

Are armholes large enough for free movement?

Are sleeves and legs short enough to prevent child's tripping or catching on them? Are tops long enough to stay tucked in?

Does garment look good?

Check for Quality:

Are seams even and flat, edges finished to prevent raveling?

Are buttons, hooks or snaps attached firmly?

How to measure for children's clothes: (use a soft tape measure)

1. **Height:** Child should stand against a wall or door jamb straight and tall in stocking feet with feet together. Place a stiff paper on top of child's head, parallel to the floor, and mark the wall. Measure from floor to the mark on the wall.
2. **Chest/bust:** Child should stand normally with arms at sides. Measure at the fullest part of the chest/bust. keep tape snug, not tight.
3. **Waist:** Child should stand normally with arms at sides. For Pants: measure where waist of pants will be worn, keep tape snug, not tight. For other garments, measure at smallest part of waist, holding tape snug, with finger between body and tape.
4. **Seat/hips:** Child should stand normally with feet together. Measure at fullest part of the seat/hips, keeping tape snug, but not tight.
5. **Inseam:** Child should stand in stocking feet with legs slightly apart. Measure from the crotch along the leg and down to the floor. Subtract $1^1/_2$ inches for garment inseam.

Infants / Toddlers: Newborn to 24 mos. Infant sizes have generous diaper allowance.

Size	Preemie	Newborn	0-3 mos.	3-6 mos.	6-9 mos.
Height (in.)	Up to 20	$20^1/_2$–22	$22^1/_2$–24	$24^1/_2$–26	$26^1/_2$–$28^1/_2$
Weight (lbs.)	Up to 5	$5^1/_2$–$8^1/_2$	9–12	$12^1/_2$–$15^1/_2$	16–19
Chest (in.)	Up to $15^1/_2$	16–$16^1/_2$	$16^1/_2$–17	17–$17^1/_2$	$17^1/_2$–18
Waist (in.)	Up to $16^1/_2$	17–$17^1/_2$	$17^1/_2$–18	18–$18^1/_2$	$18^1/_2$–19
Seat (in.)	Up to 16	$16^1/_2$–17	17–$17^1/_2$	$17^1/_2$–18	18–$18^1/_2$

Suggested wardrobe and quantity for children 0 – 24 months of age:

Outerwear:	Underwear and nightwear:	Footwear:
5 daytime outfits	48 diapers	8 pr. socks
1 jacket	6 rubber pants	1 pr. shoes
1 snowsuit	12 undershirts	1 pr. boots
6 receiving blankets	4 pajamas	**Accessories:**
1 large blanket		1 pr. mittens
		1 hat/scarf

Toddler sizes 2T-4T: Toddler sizes have less diaper allowance.

Size	12 mos.	18 mos.	24 mos.	2T	3T	4T
Height	29–$30^1/_2$	$30^1/_2$–32	$32^1/_2$–33	34–$35^1/_2$	36–$38^1/_2$	39–$41^1/_2$
Weight	$19^1/_2$–$21^1/_2$	22-24	$24^1/_2$–26	26–28	$28^1/_2$–32	$32^1/_2$–36
Chest	$18^1/_2$–19	$19^1/_2$–20	$20^1/_2$–21	$20^1/_2$–21	21–22	22–23
Waist	19–$19^1/_2$	$19^1/_2$–20	20–$20^1/_2$	20–$20^1/_2$	$20^1/_2$–21	21-$21^1/_2$
Seat	$18^1/_2$–19	$19^1/_2$–20	$20^1/_2$–21	$20^1/_2$–21	$21^1/_2$–22	$22^1/_2$–23

Preschoolers

Preschool sizes Girls 3–6X, Boys 4–7. Boys and girls have similar measurements
Slim (small frame, thin body)

Size	3	4	5	6	6X or 7
Height (in.)	36–38^1/$_2$	39–41^1/$_2$	42–44^1/$_2$	45–46^1/$_2$	47–48^1/$_2$
Weight (lbs.)	24^1/$_2$–28	28^1/$_2$–33	33^1/$_2$–38	38^1/$_2$–43	43^1/$_2$–50
Chest (in.)	20^1/$_2$–21	21^1/$_2$–22	22^1/$_2$–23	23^1/$_2$–24	24^1/$_2$–25
Waist (in.)	18^1/$_2$–19	19–19^1/$_2$	19^1/$_2$–20	20–20^1/$_2$	20^1/$_2$–21
Seat (in.)	20^1/$_2$–21	21^1/$_2$–22	22^1/$_2$–23	23^1/$_2$–24	24^1/$_2$–25

Regular (average frame and proportions)

Size	3	4	5	6	6X or 7
Height (in.)	36–38^1/$_2$	39–41^1/$_2$	42–44^1/$_2$	45–46^1/$_2$	47–48^1/$_2$
Weight (lbs.)	28^1/$_2$–32	32^1/$_2$–37	37^1/$_2$–42	42^1/$_2$–47	47^1/$_2$–54
Chest (in.)	21^1/$_2$–22	22^1/$_2$–23	23^1/$_2$–24	24^1/$_2$–25	25^1/$_2$–26
Waist (in.)	20^1/$_2$–21	21–21^1/$_2$	21^1/$_2$–22	22–22^1/$_2$	22^1/$_2$–23
Seat (in.)	21^1/$_2$–22	22^1/$_2$–23	23^1/$_2$–24	24^1/$_2$–25	25^1/$_2$–26

Suggested wardrobe and quantity for children 2–5 years of age:

Outerwear:
5 daytime outfits
1 jacket or coat
1 snowsuit
1 bathing suit

Underwear and nightwear:
8 training pants or panties
8 undershirts
2 pr. pajamas

Footwear:
8 pr. socks
1 pr. shoes
1 pr. boots
Accessories:
1 pr. mittens
1 hat/scarf

Boys Slim: 8 to 20 Slim Small frame, thin body

Size	8	9	10	11	12	14	16	18	20
Height (in.)	47^1/$_2$–50^1/$_2$	51–52^1/$_2$	51–54^1/$_2$	55–56^1/$_2$	55–58^1/$_2$	59–61^1/$_2$	62–64^1/$_2$	65–66^1/$_2$	67–68^1/$_2$
Chest (in.)	24^1/$_2$–26	26–26^1/$_2$	26^1/$_2$–27^1/$_2$	27–28	28–29	29^1/$_2$–30^1/$_2$	31–32	32^1/$_2$–33^1/$_2$	24–35
Waist (in.)	21–22	22–22^1/$_2$	22^1/$_2$–23	23–23^1/$_2$	23^1/$_2$–24	24^1/$_2$–25	25^1/$_2$–26	26^1/$_2$–27	27/$_2$–28
Seat (in.)	24^1/$_2$–27	26–26^1/$_2$	26^1/$_2$–27^1/$_2$	27–28	28–29	29^1/$_2$–30^1/$_2$	31–32^1/$_2$	33–34	34^1/$_2$–35^1/$_2$
Inseam (in.)	21	22^1/$_4$	23^1/$_2$	24^1/$_2$	26	27^1/$_2$	29	29^3/$_4$	30^1/$_2$

Suggested wardrobe and quantity for boys 6–12 years of age:

Outerwear:
1 heavy coat
1 jacket
1 dress shirt/tie
4 polo shirts
1 raincoat
2 pr. shorts
1 sweater
1 pr. slacks
3 pr. jeans
1 bathing suit

Underwear and nightwear:
7 undershorts or briefs
7 undershirts
2 pr. pajamas

Footwear:
8 pr. socks
1 pr. school shoes
1 pr. sneakers
1 pr. boots

Accessories:
1 hat
1 belt
Gloves/mittens

Boys Husky:

Size	8H	10H	12H	14H	16H	18H	20H	22H	24H
Height (in.)	49–50¹/₂	51–53	53¹/₂–55¹/₂	56–58	58¹/₂–60	59¹/₂–61	60¹/₂–62	61¹/₂–63	62¹/₂–64
Chest (in.)	28–29	29¹/₂–30¹/₂	31–32	32¹/₂–34	34¹/₂–35	35¹/₂–36	36¹/₂–37	37¹/₂–38	38¹/₂–39
Waist (in.)	26–26¹/₂	27–27¹/₂	28–28¹/₂	29–29¹/₂	30–30¹/₂	31–31¹/₂	32–32¹/₂	33–33¹/₂	34–34¹/₂
Seat (in.)	28¹/₂–29¹/₂	30–31	31¹/₂–32¹/₂	33–34¹/₂	35–36	36¹/₂–37	37¹/₂–38	38¹/₂–39	39¹/₂–40
Inseam	21	22¹/₄	24¹/₂	25¹/₂	27	27¹/₂	28	28¹/₂	29

Boys Regular:

Size	8	9	10	11	12	14	16	18	20
Height (in.)	47–50¹/₂	51–52¹/₂	51–54¹/₂	55–56¹/₂	55–58¹/₂	59–61¹/₂	62–64¹/₂	65–64¹/₂	67–68¹/₂
Chest (in.)	26–27	27–27¹/₂	27¹/₂–28¹/₂	28¹/₂–29	29–30	30¹/₂–32	32¹/₂–33¹/₂	34–35	35¹/₂–36¹/₂
Waist (in.)	23–24	24–24¹/₂	24¹/₂–25	25–25¹/₂	25¹/₂–26	26¹/₂–27	27¹/₂–28	28¹/₂–29	29¹/₂–30
Seat (in.)	25¹/₂–27	27–27¹/₂	27¹/₂–28¹/₂	28¹/₂–29	29–30	30¹/₂–32	32¹/₂–34	34¹/₂–35¹/₂	36–37
Inseam	21	22¹/₄	23¹/₂	24¹/₂	26	27¹/₂	29	29¹/₂	30¹/₂

Girls Slim: 7 to 16 slim (small frame, thin body)

Size	7	8	10	12	14	16
Height (in.)	50–51¹/₂	52–53¹/₂	54–55¹/₂	56–58	58¹/₂–60¹/₂	61–63
Bust (in.)	24–25	25–26	26¹/₂–27¹/₂	28–29	29¹/₂–30¹/₂	31–32
Waist (in.)	20¹/₂–21	21–21¹/₂	22–22¹/₂	23–23¹/₂	24–24¹/₂	25–25¹/₂
Hips (in.)	25¹/₂–26	26–27	27¹/₂–28¹/₂	29–30¹/₂	31–32¹/₂	33–34¹/₂

Girls Regular: 7 to 18 regular (average frame and proportions)

Size	7	8	10	12	14	16	18
Height (in.)	50–51¹/₂	52–53¹/₂	54–55¹/₂	56–58	58¹/₂–60¹/₂	61–63	63¹/₂–65¹/₂
Bust (in.)	25¹/₂–26¹/₂	26¹/₂–27¹/₂	28–29	29¹/₂–30¹/₂	31–32	32¹/₂–33¹/₂	34–35
Waist (in.)	22¹/₂–23	23–23¹/₂	24–24¹/₂	25–25¹/₂	26–26¹/₂	27–27¹/₂	28–28¹/₂
Hips (in.)	27¹/₂–28	28–29	29¹/₂–30¹/₂	31–32¹/₂	33–34¹/₂	35–36¹/₂	37–38¹/₂

Girls Plus: Girls Plus 10¹/₂ to 20¹/₂ (fuller body in proportion to height)

Size	10¹/₂	12¹/₂	14¹/₂	16¹/₂	18¹/₂	20¹/₂
Height (in.)	54–55¹/₂	56–58	58¹/₂–60¹/₂	61–63	61¹/₂–63¹/₂	61¹/₂–63¹/₂
Bust (in.)	30¹/₂–31¹/₂	32–33	33¹/₂–34¹/₂	35–36	36¹/₂–38	38¹/₂–40
Waist (in.)	27¹/₂–28	28¹/₂–29	29¹/₂–30	30¹/₂–31	31¹/₂–33	33¹/₂–35
Hips (in.)	32¹/₂–33¹/₂	34–35¹/₂	36–37¹/₂	38–39¹/₂	40–41¹/₂	42–43¹/₂

Girls tights/pantyhose

Size	4–6x (S)	7–10 (M)	12–14 (L)
Weight (lbs.)	32¹/₂–54 lbs.	52¹/₂–74¹/₂ lbs.	75–96 lbs.
Height (in.)	39–48¹/₂	49–55¹/₂	56–60¹/₂

Girls bodysuits/leotards

Size	4–5	6–7	8–10	12–14
Weight (lbs.)	32¹/₂–42	42¹/₂–60	60¹/₂–74	75–96
Height (in.)	39–44¹/₂	45–51¹/₂	52–55¹/₂	56–60¹/₂

Suggested wardrobe and quantity for girls 6–12 years of age:

Outerwear:
1 heavy coat
1 raincoat
1 jacket
1 sweater
2 dresses
1 skirt
1 blouse
3 shirts
1 pr. jeans
2 pr. slacks
2 pr. shorts
1 bathing suit

Underwear and nightwear:
1 slip
8 pr. panties
1 bathrobe
2 pr. pajamas or nighties

Older girls from 13-18 years of age also need: 3 bras

Footwear:
6 pr. socks
2 pr. tights
1 pr. school shoes
1 pr. sneakers
1 pr. boots
1 pr. slippers

Accessories
1 pr. gloves/mittens
1 hat/scarf
1 belt

Teen Boys: Average frame to proportions. Height 5'3" to 5'10"

Size	26 waist	27 waist	28 waist	29 waist	30 waist
Chest (in.)	30¹/₂–31¹/₂	31¹/₂–32¹/₂	32¹/₂–33¹/₂	33¹/₂–34¹/₂	34¹/₂–35¹/₂
Waist (in.)	25–26	26–27	27–28	28–29	29–30
Seat (in.)	31¹/₂–32¹/₂	32¹/₂–33¹/₂	33¹/₂–34¹/₂	34¹/₂–35¹/₂	35¹/₂–36¹/₂
Inseam (in.)	28	28	28	28	30
	30	30	30	30	32
		32	32	32	

My Child's Measurement Record

Child should be measured twice a year, every six months, unless rapid growth is noted. Size changes are least costly when done with seasonal changes in clothes.

Age _____

Date					Shoe size
Height					
Weight					
Chest/Bust					
Waist					
Seat/Hips					
Inseam					
Size					

Age _____

Date					Shoe size
Height					
Weight					
Chest/Bust					
Waist					
Seat/Hips					
Inseam					
Size					

Age _____

Date					Shoe size
Height					
Weight					
Chest/Bust					
Waist					
Seat/Hips					
Inseam					
Size					

Child should be measured twice a year, every six months, unless rapid growth is noted. Size changes are least costly when done with seasonal changes in clothes.

Age _____

Date					Shoe size
Height					
Weight					
Chest/Bust					
Waist					
Seat/Hips					
Inseam					
Size					

Age _____

Date					Shoe size
Height					
Weight					
Chest/Bust					
Waist					
Seat/Hips					
Inseam					
Size					

Age _____

Date					Shoe size
Height					
Weight					
Chest/Bust					
Waist					
Seat/Hips					
Inseam					
Size					

Inventory of My Child's Toys

When your child receives a toy as a gift, they should write a thank-you letter to the donor if they are at least five years old. While they may not write perfectly, the act of thanking someone for a gift is a necessary social activity. As your child gets older, writing letters is increasingly important in helping them put thoughts on paper. For each occasion that your child receives a gift, make a note of who gave the gift and what it was. Check off when your child has written a thank-you. The thank-you should be written within the week.

The Parent/Teen Safe Living Contract

By signing this contract, parents and teenagers show each other their commitment to a safe, drug-free lifestyle. Teenagers understand that they are expected to obey the laws regarding the use of alcohol and other drugs. Any individual whose signature is on this document agrees that he or she has read, understood and agreed to uphold each of the positive life choices expressed below.

For Teenagers:

- Because I know my parents are concerned about my safety, I will make sure to let them know where I am going and when I will be home.
- I will feel free to call home to be picked up at any hour and from any place rather than get into a car with a driver who has been drinking or using drugs. If there is no one at home to pick me up, my parents agree to pay for a taxi or other available transportation.
- Whether I am the driver or a passenger, I will always wear my safety belt while in a moving car.
- I agree to participate in family counsel meetings when requested.

Signature_____ Date_____

For Parents:

- In case my family needs to reach me for an emergency, I will make sure to let them know where I am going and when I will be home.
- I will not drink to excess or use illicit drugs. I will not drink alcohol in situations where its effects might put others or me at risk.
- I will not drink and drive, nor will I get into a car with a driver who has had too much to drink.
- I agree to pick my child up from any place and at any time, no questions asked at that time, in order to ensure that my child gets home safely.
- Whether I am the driver or a passenger, I will always wear my safety belt while in a moving car.
- I will not allow alcohol or drugs to be available to young people in my home at any time.
- I agree to be home to supervise any gatherings held for young people in my home.

Signature_____ Date_____

Television Viewing Log

Name: _____   Week of: _____

	Time	Program	Channel	Hours
Sunday:	_____	_____	_____	_____
	_____	_____	_____	_____
	_____	_____	_____	_____
	_____	_____	_____	_____
Monday:	_____	_____	_____	_____
	_____	_____	_____	_____
	_____	_____	_____	_____
	_____	_____	_____	_____
Tuesday:	_____	_____	_____	_____
	_____	_____	_____	_____
	_____	_____	_____	_____
	_____	_____	_____	_____
Wednesday:	_____	_____	_____	_____
	_____	_____	_____	_____
	_____	_____	_____	_____
	_____	_____	_____	_____
Thursday:	_____	_____	_____	_____
	_____	_____	_____	_____
	_____	_____	_____	_____
	_____	_____	_____	_____
Friday:	_____	_____	_____	_____
	_____	_____	_____	_____
	_____	_____	_____	_____
	_____	_____	_____	_____
Saturday:	_____	_____	_____	_____
	_____	_____	_____	_____
	_____	_____	_____	_____
	_____	_____	_____	_____

Total Hours: _____

Name: _____   Week of: _____

	Time	Program	Channel	Hours
Sunday:	_____	_____	_____	_____
	_____	_____	_____	_____
	_____	_____	_____	_____
	_____	_____	_____	_____
Monday:	_____	_____	_____	_____
	_____	_____	_____	_____
	_____	_____	_____	_____
	_____	_____	_____	_____
Tuesday:	_____	_____	_____	_____
	_____	_____	_____	_____
	_____	_____	_____	_____
	_____	_____	_____	_____
Wednesday:	_____	_____	_____	_____
	_____	_____	_____	_____
	_____	_____	_____	_____
	_____	_____	_____	_____
Thursday:	_____	_____	_____	_____
	_____	_____	_____	_____
	_____	_____	_____	_____
	_____	_____	_____	_____
Friday:	_____	_____	_____	_____
	_____	_____	_____	_____
	_____	_____	_____	_____
	_____	_____	_____	_____
Saturday:	_____	_____	_____	_____
	_____	_____	_____	_____
	_____	_____	_____	_____
	_____	_____	_____	_____

Total Hours: _____

Rules for Family Meetings

Equal Voice: Each member of the family in a democracy has an equal voice in the decisions made. Children need to feel that they belong as a member of the family and they can make a difference in what the family decides to do.

Speak Up: It is important that every person is encouraged to participate and say what he or she thinks or feel about what is being discussed. Even the negative comments can be helpful.

Reaching Decisions: Discuss the item so that everyone has spoken their turn. When there is a disagreement, the item can be tabled until the next meeting, giving everyone time to think more about it, or the parent may make a decision as head of the household to try it for awhile and re-discuss the progress at a later meeting.

Decisions: All the decisions made at a meeting should be carried out until the next meeting, when they can be discussed again if necessary. Complaints after the meeting about decisions made can be responded to by saying: "We will discuss this again at our next family meeting."

The family meeting is not a place to fight, yell or get out of control. A meeting can be stopped if the emotions are getting out of control and resumed when persons can discuss the problems to resolve them in a democratic manner.

How to get started with Family Meetings

1. Parents call the meeting. All family members gather at a special time during the week to sit down together and discuss the family issues. This should be a time without distractions and appointments.

2. A chairperson is needed. Usually, the oldest member of the family starts out as chair, but everyone should have a chance to be chair. The responsibility of the chair is to keep the discussion focused and see that everyone's opinion is heard.

3. A secretary is needed. The secretary takes notes during the meeting, writes up the minutes (or agreements) and reads them at the next meeting. Parents can start this role, but other family members should take turns at this in an agreed-upon order, so that no one person is in charge every time.

Agenda for the Family Meeting

☐ 1. The meeting should begin on a positive note by telling the good things that have happened and should be recognized. This is the time for family members to say "thanks" to each other for good deeds done or for help given during the past week and to recognize strengths and encourage improvement.

☐ 2. Minutes are read. Last week's secretary reads the minutes from the last meeting.

☐ 3. Old Business. Topics unfinished at the last meeting can be discussed further now.

☐ 4. Finances: This is a special time to discuss financial matters. This is also a good time to pass out allowances.

☐ 5. New Business: Discussion of new topics, complaints or problems on the agenda.

☐ 6. Treat: The meeting adjourns, but the family stays together for a game, an outing or a snack. This is an opportunity to have fun together, to enjoy each other's company and to get the week off to a good start!

Communication tips:

Speak respectfully

Invite everyone's ideas

Share how you think and feel

Ask yourself how others feel

Compliment others

Don't put anyone's ideas down

Don't interrupt

Don't monopolize the discussion

Don't consider only your point of view

Don't criticize others

Don't call anyone names

Family Communication

Family communication is as important as any corporate communication. Sometimes it is necessary in a corporation to call a meeting to clarify policies and procedures. Meetings are a fundamental practice to explain to individuals what their job responsibilities are and how their actions are affecting other staff members. Is it time for a corporate meeting of your family? How does your family communicate with each other? Try asking these questions in your family meetings. Compare your answers.

1. **What are our goals as a family? Here are a few examples to help you begin.**

Succeed at home first	Keep a sense of humor
Seek a Spiritual faith	Be sincere
Be honest and trustworthy	Learn new things
Hear both sides before making a judgment	Help the weak or poor
Plan for tomorrow	Keep a positive attitude
Always keep promises	Be patient with others
Be orderly	Save money and budget carefully
Help others	Seek adventure
Cheer others when they are feeling down	Don't worry about the future
Impress others	Do well at work or school
Make friends	Study family history
Practice a healthy lifestyle	Learn to problem solve
Get more self-esteem	Serve the community

2. What are your individual goals? Do your personal goals contribute to the family goals? Are family members helping each other to achieve their individual goals?

3. What is your role as a family unit? Do you work together or does everyone do his or her own thing? Do you support one another or tear each other down?

4. What household chores are expected of you regularly? What is your job description at home? Who takes out the garbage? Who does the dishes? When? Does everyone know what part they play in the everyday operation of running a house?

5. What responsibilities do you have to other members of your family? Is there a curfew? What limitations are placed on family members? What time are you supposed to be home from work or school before it becomes necessary to call?

6. What kinds of rules should the family have about friends coming over? Taking the car? Staying with?

7. What makes you want to come home?

8. What embarrasses you?

9. What should be our family's highest priorities?

10. What would you like the family to do together?

Some Topics of Problems or Concerns for Families

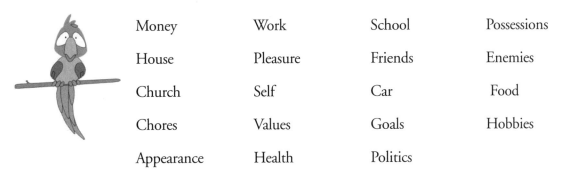

Money	Work	School	Possessions
House	Pleasure	Friends	Enemies
Church	Self	Car	Food
Chores	Values	Goals	Hobbies
Appearance	Health	Politics	

Circle those topics you feel you need to discuss with your family. Choose one of the topics to begin at the next family meeting. Make notes of concerns and possible ways to resolve them.

Places to Go

Ideas	Name	Location	Cost
Museums:	_____	_____	$_____
Nature Parks:	_____	_____	$_____
Zoos:	_____	_____	$_____
Amusement Parks:	_____	_____	$_____
Famous Buildings:	_____	_____	$_____
Monuments:	_____	_____	$_____
Rivers:	_____	_____	$_____
Lakes:	_____	_____	$_____
Oceans:	_____	_____	$_____
Famous Sights:	_____	_____	$_____
Places to Eat:	_____	_____	$_____
Concerts:	_____	_____	$_____
Clubs:	_____	_____	$_____
Festivals:	_____	_____	$_____
Arts and Craft Fairs:	_____	_____	$_____
Spectator Sports:	_____	_____	$_____

Use a form like this for family meeting minutes. (You can use an old notebook)

Date: _____

Chairman: _____

Secretary: _____

Old Business:

_____

_____

_____

Finances: _____

Allowance can be dollars according to age, a set amount or negotiated,

New Business:

_____

_____

_____

_____

_____

_____

_____

_____

_____

_____

_____

Establishing Rules

Do not make rules that you cannot enforce!

☐ A rule must be clear and specific.

☐ A rule must deal with a specific action by the child that the parent can see.

☐ A rule must have a consequence that the parent is prepared to follow through on.

☐ A rule must offer a choice: responsibility or restriction.

Putting rules in writing when you have the family meetings will help all family members work together. The rules can be posted on the refrigerator or on a door. You can get creative and make a nice poster with the rules neatly printed out and decorated. Rules are sometimes different for different children because of age, maturity, abilities and special needs. Don't make any rules unless you need them.

Examples:

Consequences for non-compliance:

1. Bedtimes (in bed, lights out)
   Joe age 15, 10:00 p.m.
   Amy age 12, 9:30 p.m.
   Rob age 9, 8:30 p.m.

   must go to bed 15 min. earlier next night

2. Evening curfew:
   Joe, 9:00 p.m.
   Amy, 8:30 p.m.
   Rob, 7:30 p.m.

   Curfew set earlier by the number of minutes late, for one week.

3. Away from home rules:
   Parents must know where you are at all times.

   Grounding

4. Chores:
   Breakfast – everyone rinses out own dishes and cleans up their own spot.
   Dinner dishes – wash and dry
   Joe and Amy, Mon, Wed.
   Rob and Mom, Tues., Thurs.
   Joe and Dad, Fri.
   Mom and Amy, Sat.

   If chore is not done, you take one of Mom or Dad's chores for a day the next day.

5. Yard Chores:
   Grass cut and raked by noon, Sat.
   Snow shoveled within 4 hours

   $5.00 allowance paid to person who did chore if not done by assigned person.

6. School Work
   Finish homework before TV, phone

   No TV or phone on following night

7. Problems with grades   Priorities set after each report card.

8. Extra-curricular activities (teens)
   Teens should participate in at least one formal extra-curricular activity involving at least two practices, rehearsals, or meetings per week, or have an after-school job.

9. Respecting the rights of others:

No swearing	$1 per swear word used
No insulting names	$2 per word
No borrowing without permission	Person wronged will set consequence
No punching or hitting	Sent to separate rooms
Quiet down when asked	Sent to room

10. Youngest children have priority on TV, electronic games, etc. after dinner until bath time and bed.

11. Rules about car:

Teens replenish gas used	Loss of car privileges
No one else drives car	Duration to be determined.
Not allowed in any car if driver has been drinking	Loss of license for one year

12. No friends in house when parents are not home.   No friends can visit, duration to be determined.

You are responsible for your friend's conduct when in our home. (You make the rules and write them out, so everyone can understand them.)

You do not need to nag, scold or hassle children. If the situation is important to you, make a rule about it. There are natural consequences which children need to learn also. If they leave their skates out in the rain, they will be ruined. Rules help everyone to understand and agree on what is expected. When we have rules, we have more cooperation and can act responsibly.

Medical Consent Form

This form is authorization by parents for another to consent to hospitalization, surgery or special medical procedures during absence of parents.

Name of Mother: _____

Work address: _____   Phone: _____

_____

Name of Father: _____

Work address: _____   Phone: _____

_____

1. Name of child: _____ Birth date:_____ Allergies: _____
    Father's name: _____

2. Name of child: _____ Birth date:_____ Allergies: _____
    Father's name: _____

3. Name of child: _____ Birth date:_____ Allergies: _____
    Father's name: _____

4. Name of child: _____ Birth date:_____ Allergies: _____
    Father's name: _____

We hereby appoint: Name _____   Phone:_____

Address: _____

City, State, Zip_____

As the person who, during my/our absence from _____, shall be authorized to consent for all medical and/or surgical treatment and/or special procedures (including by way of illustration and not limitation, administration of anesthesia, blood transfusions, diagnostic tests, etc.) which may be required during our absence. Without in any manner limiting the foregoing appointment and authorization, if circumstances permit, I/we would like to have our doctor consulted in connection with such medical and/or surgical treatment and/or special procedures. Emergency care, its officers and personnel and any physician providing care are authorized by the above named to act as appointed with the same force and effect as if personally executed by us.

Doctor: _____   Phone: _____

In consideration of the services which are rendered to any child named above, pursuant hereto, we agree to pay for all such services. This authorization shall be effective until _____ year _____or until revoked in writing.

Signed_____   Signed _____

In the event that this form is executed by only one parent, please state below the reason why the signature of the other parent cannot be obtained_____

_____

_____

Parenting Emergency Information Form

1. Child's name:_____
   Date of Birth: _____

2. Address and directions to our home: _____
   _____
   _____

3. Home phone number:_____

4. Neighbor or relative's name and phone number:
   _____
   _____

5. Doctor's name/ address / phone:
   _____
   _____

6. Poison Control center phone: _____

7. Directions to nearest hospital: _____
   _____

8. Insurance information: _____ Number: _____
   Child's ID number:_____

9. Child's allergies: _____
   _____

10. Regular medicine child is taking: _____
    _____

11. Date of last Tetanus booster: _____

12. Dietary restrictions, if any:_____

13. Past history of serious illness or injury:_____
    _____
    _____

    Other important information: _____
    _____
    _____

Fill out the information on this sheet for each child and keep it. Your babysitter should be able to take it, along with a power of attorney, in case of an emergency with your child. Remember, this information is vital and could save your child's life!

Records of Birth

Name: _____ Sex: _____

Mother's Name: _____

Father's Name: _____

Birth Date: _____ Time of Birth: _____

Place of Birth: _____

Name of Hospital: _____

Address: _____ Phone: _____

Attending Physician: _____

Birth weight: _____lbs. oz. Length: _____inches

Hair Color: _____ Eye Color: _____

Blood Type: _____

Birthmarks/distinguishing traits: _____

Namesake: _____

Relevant Information: _____

_____

_____

_____

Name: _____ Sex: _____

Mother's Name: _____

Father's Name: _____

Birth Date: _____ Time of Birth: _____

Place of Birth: _____

Name of Hospital: _____

Address: _____ Phone: _____

Attending Physician: _____

Birth weight: _____lbs. oz. Length: _____inches

Hair Color: _____ Eye Color: _____

Blood Type: _____

Birthmarks/distinguishing traits: _____

Namesake: _____

Relevant Information: _____

_____

_____

_____

Record of Attendance

Name: _____   Date: _____

Place of Attendance:_____

	Jan.	Feb.	Mar.	Apr.	May	Jun.	Jul.	Aug.	Sep.	Oct.	Nov.	Dec.
1	—	—	—	—	—	—	—	—	—	—	—	—
2	—	—	—	—	—	—	—	—	—	—	—	—
3	—	—	—	—	—	—	—	—	—	—	—	—
4	—	—	—	—	—	—	—	—	—	—	—	—
5	—	—	—	—	—	—	—	—	—	—	—	—
6	—	—	—	—	—	—	—	—	—	—	—	—
7	—	—	—	—	—	—	—	—	—	—	—	—
8	—	—	—	—	—	—	—	—	—	—	—	—
9	—	—	—	—	—	—	—	—	—	—	—	—
10	—	—	—	—	—	—	—	—	—	—	—	—
11	—	—	—	—	—	—	—	—	—	—	—	—
12	—	—	—	—	—	—	—	—	—	—	—	—
13	—	—	—	—	—	—	—	—	—	—	—	—
14	—	—	—	—	—	—	—	—	—	—	—	—
15	—	—	—	—	—	—	—	—	—	—	—	—
16	—	—	—	—	—	—	—	—	—	—	—	—
17	—	—	—	—	—	—	—	—	—	—	—	—
18	—	—	—	—	—	—	—	—	—	—	—	—
19	—	—	—	—	—	—	—	—	—	—	—	—
20	—	—	—	—	—	—	—	—	—	—	—	—
21	—	—	—	—	—	—	—	—	—	—	—	—
22	—	—	—	—	—	—	—	—	—	—	—	—
23	—	—	—	—	—	—	—	—	—	—	—	—
24	—	—	—	—	—	—	—	—	—	—	—	—
25	—	—	—	—	—	—	—	—	—	—	—	—
26	—	—	—	—	—	—	—	—	—	—	—	—
27	—	—	—	—	—	—	—	—	—	—	—	—
28	—	—	—	—	—	—	—	—	—	—	—	—
29	—	—	—	—	—	—	—	—	—	—	—	—
30	—	—	—	—	—	—	—	—	—	—	—	—
31	—	—	—	—	—	—	—	—	—	—	—	—
Total:	—	—	—	—	—	—	—	—	—	—	—	—

Record of Attendance

Name: _____ Date: _____

Place of Attendance: _____

	Jan.	Feb.	Mar.	Apr.	May	Jun.	Jul.	Aug.	Sep.	Oct.	Nov.	Dec.
1	____	____	____	____	____	____	____	____	____	____	____	____
2	____	____	____	____	____	____	____	____	____	____	____	____
3	____	____	____	____	____	____	____	____	____	____	____	____
4	____	____	____	____	____	____	____	____	____	____	____	____
5	____	____	____	____	____	____	____	____	____	____	____	____
6	____	____	____	____	____	____	____	____	____	____	____	____
7	____	____	____	____	____	____	____	____	____	____	____	____
8	____	____	____	____	____	____	____	____	____	____	____	____
9	____	____	____	____	____	____	____	____	____	____	____	____
10	____	____	____	____	____	____	____	____	____	____	____	____
11	____	____	____	____	____	____	____	____	____	____	____	____
12	____	____	____	____	____	____	____	____	____	____	____	____
13	____	____	____	____	____	____	____	____	____	____	____	____
14	____	____	____	____	____	____	____	____	____	____	____	____
15	____	____	____	____	____	____	____	____	____	____	____	____
16	____	____	____	____	____	____	____	____	____	____	____	____
17	____	____	____	____	____	____	____	____	____	____	____	____
18	____	____	____	____	____	____	____	____	____	____	____	____
19	____	____	____	____	____	____	____	____	____	____	____	____
20	____	____	____	____	____	____	____	____	____	____	____	____
21	____	____	____	____	____	____	____	____	____	____	____	____
22	____	____	____	____	____	____	____	____	____	____	____	____
23	____	____	____	____	____	____	____	____	____	____	____	____
24	____	____	____	____	____	____	____	____	____	____	____	____
25	____	____	____	____	____	____	____	____	____	____	____	____
26	____	____	____	____	____	____	____	____	____	____	____	____
27	____	____	____	____	____	____	____	____	____	____	____	____
28	____	____	____	____	____	____	____	____	____	____	____	____
29	____	____	____	____	____	____	____	____	____	____	____	____
30	____	____	____	____	____	____	____	____	____	____	____	____
31	____	____	____	____	____	____	____	____	____	____	____	____
Total:	____	____	____	____	____	____	____	____	____	____	____	____

Child Care Services

Caregiver's Name: _____ Rate/hr: $_____ /week: _____

How long in business? _____ Education: _____

Address: _____

_____ Phone: _____

Days/hours available: _____ Ages accepted: _____

References: _____

Additional Information: _____

Are drop-ins accepted_____ Is there special care?_____ Are meals or snacks provided?_____

Is there a discount for another child? Full or part of day? _____

Caregiver's Name: _____ Rate/hr: $_____ /week: _____

How long in business? _____ Education: _____

Address: _____

_____ Phone: _____

Days/hours available: _____ Ages accepted: _____

References: _____

Additional Information: _____

Are drop-ins accepted_____ Is there special care?_____ Are meals or snacks provided?_____

Is there a discount for another child? Full or part of day? _____

Caregiver's Name: _____ Rate/hr: $_____ /week: _____

How long in business? _____ Education: _____

Address: _____

_____ Phone: _____

Days/hours available: _____ Ages accepted: _____

References: _____

Additional Information: _____

Are drop-ins accepted_____ Is there special care?_____ Are meals or snacks provided?_____

Is there a discount for another child? Full or part of day? _____

Other questions you may want to ask:

What is the policy when a child becomes sick?

Is there transportation available?

What items are needed for the child every day?

Have any children been injured by other children at the daycare?

Copy this page for the Sitter!

Important Phone Numbers:

Fire _____   Police _____

Doctor _____   Office no: _____

Hospital _____

Parent's location: _____

Phone number: _____

Time Expected Back: _____

If parents cannot be reached, call this number: _____

Special instructions: _____

_____

_____

_____

_____

_____

_____

_____

Bedtime is: _____

My Pregnancy History

Maintain this information for each pregnancy.

I found out I was pregnant when _____

I began getting morning sickness on _____ and it continued through
_____.

Other symptoms I had: _____

My beginning weight was: _____ My delivery weight was: _____

I first felt the baby move when: _____

The doctor gave specific recommendations for: _____
_____

1st month: _____

2nd month: _____

3rd month: _____

4th month: _____

5th month: _____

6th month: _____

7th month: _____

8th month: _____

9th month: _____

Total number of days to delivery: _____

Delivery was natural _____ cesarean _____

After delivery problems: _____
_____
_____

Home Management

SECTION

7

Home Organization

The Bathroom:
- What needs to be put around the tub/shower area so that soap, shampoo, conditioner, towels and washcloths, non-slip mats, bath mats, etc., are in easy reach when needed?
- How can I organize my linen closet so that the towels, washcloths, toilet paper, soap, etc is easily seen and reached?
- How can I organize my makeup so that it is easily reached and I have the mirror and lighting I need?
- Where can I store the cleaning items needed for the bathroom, the toilet brush, plunger, toilet paper, cleanser, etc.?
- Are there hooks or hangers to put robes, clothes, for dressing area space?

The Bedroom:
- What needs to be organized so that the sheets, blankets, and pillows are easily reached when needed and out of sight when not needed?
- How do I organize my closet so that the clothing stays clean and reachable and I can dress in a hurry when needed?
- Is there space in the bedroom for laying out clothes? Where is the space for pressing clothes? Where is the space for seasonal clothing?

The Kitchen:
- What space is needed for the pantry? Do I need shelves, boxes, a closet or cupboards?
- When I prepare food, I need those items I will be using close at hand. Where can I store these things?
- Where will I store the things I do not use every day, like Christmas things?
- What would be the easiest way to store the glassware, dishes, pots and pans, other cookware?
- How easy is it to wash the dishes?
- Where do I store the soap, cleaners, mops and brooms for the kitchen?
- Where can I keep my recipe books?

The Living Room:
- How am I going to store the videos/CDs so that they are not lying all over?
- Is the TV easily seen when I want to watch it?
- Is there comfortable furniture to sit on when I talk to friends or want to relax?
- Where is the phone? Is there a table so that a pencil and paper are handy? Where are the phone books stored? Where do I pay the bills and keep my records?

The Craft Room:
- How do I store my hobbies, games, toys, so that they are reachable when I need them? Should I use a closet for these things or do I need more space than that?

Home Management

Toddlers and preschoolers enjoy increased physical agility, but haven't yet developed the judgment needed to keep their impulses in check! In addition to the basic safety precautions you took while they were babies — such as installing locks on kitchen cabinets and tying blind cords up high—you'll need to keep ahead of these busy little minds by anticipating that, to a two-year-old, the VCR slot looks like a toaster and the bookcases are similar in concept to the local jungle gym. If possible, provide your child with an area where she can safely jump, climb and play pretend games and make certain areas of the house (storage areas and entertainment and sewing rooms, for example) are off-limits except for special, closely supervised occasions.

Also, install smoke and carbon monoxide detectors on every level of your home, especially in the bedrooms. And be sure to change the batteries regularly.

General Safety:
1. Are guns and other firearms stored in a locked cabinet so that children cannot get to them?
2. Is food prepared and cared for adequately? Hot foods hot, and cold foods cold, and food not left out at room temperature to develop contamination and make the family ill?
3. Are dishes cleaned appropriately after each meal?
4. Are the floors clean enough for children to sit on? (Animal droppings should be cleaned up immediately.)
5. Are all broken windows cleaned out of shards of glass immediately?

Make it Safe to Walk:
1. Do rugs, runners and mats in the house have nonskid backings or are taped to floor so that no one can trip on them?
2. Are traffic areas, stairs, entrances and the kitchen free of obstacles like low furniture, toys and newspapers and clothes?
3. Are stairways lighted so the edges of steps can be seen easily going up or down?
4. Are sturdy handrails fastened securely to structural supports on both sides of the stairway?
5. Are stair treads or carpeting tacked down securely? (Nails should not protrude.) Install nonskid treads on steep or slippery staircases.
6. Do family members avoid wearing socks, smooth-soled shoes or slippers on stairs, which could cause a slip and a serious fall?
7. Are stairways clear? (Nothing should be stored on the stairs.)

    Teach your child to use the stairs after she's been walking for a few months and is steady on her feet, not while she's still wobbling.

    Block stairs at the top and bottom with childproof gates. Avoid pressure-mounted gates, which can pop off unexpectedly, and accordion-style models that can entangle clothing and trap heads and fingers. Hardware-mounted models that screw into the wall are the best (you may want to hire a pro to help you install one).

8. Make sure your childproof gate openings are too small for kids' hands and feet.

Doors
Don't let children play near doors. Small fingers can get caught in doors both near the hinge and on the knob side. If the locks on your bathroom and bedroom doors do not have emergency releases on the outside, either cover or remove them; children can easily lock themselves in.

Windows
Use lockable safety catches, also known as window guards, to keep children inside and to prevent strangers from reaching in. Available at hardware stores, these catches let you open the window a set amount (generally six inches).

Also, remember that screens are not enough to keep a child from falling out of a window. If you live in the upper floors of an apartment building, child-safety bars (easily removable in case of fire) are essential and are even required by law in some states.

Safe Living Room

- Tack down scatter rugs with double-backed tape or remove them.
- Wedge books, CDs, tapes, etc., tightly in their shelves.
- If you have wooden floors, make sure your child wears slip-resistant shoes or slippers.
- Keep scissors, pens, needles and other sharp household implements in a locked drawer.
1. Are chimneys cleaned when necessary to control for build-up from burning wood?
2. Are heaters with 3-prong plugs being used in a 3-hole outlet or with a properly attached-grounded adapter?
3. Are heaters and stoves placed where they won't be knocked over, and away from curtains, rugs and other flammable materials?
4. Are kerosene or gas heaters only used when everyone in the family is awake and the room is ventilated to avoid carbon monoxide poisoning?

Dining Room

- Lock your liquor cabinets.
- Select your highchair carefully—if you can open the safety buckle easily, it's likely that your two-year-old can too.
- Avoid tablecloths, which are an invitation to disaster—one tug and dinner is on the floor.
- Serve your child's food on non-breakable dishes.
- Keep fragile china and glass out of reach and locked away in a cabinet or breakfront.

Kitchen Safety

- When cooking on the stovetop, turn the handles on pots and pans inward, away from the front, and do all cooking on back burners. Remember that hot liquid can scald for up to half an hour after they reach the boiling point.
- Use safety guards around the stovetop. Keep household cleaners and chemicals out of reach; buy products with child-resistant tops. Keep the dishwasher door locked when not in use. When loading it, place knives with their blades down. Install locks on your oven and refrigerator if you need to keep your child out.
- Never leave plastic bags lying around; they can suffocate a child.
1. Is the stove properly vented, and the vent free of built-up grease that can catch fire?
2. Are potholders, curtains, and other flammable items kept away from the stovetop and oven?
3. Do family members avoid wearing loose-fitting garments with long sleeves, like bathrobes, when cooking that can easily catch fire, or tip over pots, causing burns?
4. Is a home fire extinguisher nearby and has it been checked regularly to make sure the pressure is adequate? Remember that water won't put out grease or electrical fires!
5. Is the water temperature 120° or lower to prevent burns?
6. Are household cleaning agents stored out of reach of children, or are safety latches on cabinet doors or drawers?
7. Are non-food items in their original containers clearly marked and stored separately from food, so that a child would not eat it?

Safety in the Bathroom

- Cover the bathtub spout to prevent heads from getting bumped. Keep the temperature regulator on your hot water heater to 120 degrees F. Run cold water first in the tub or sink, then add hot water to warm it up (helps prevent scalding).
- Apply textured strips to the surface of tubs or showers or use nonskid mats.
- **Never leave children under five in the bathtub unattended.**
- Empty the bathtub immediately after use. A child can drown in as little as one inch of water.
- Lock up all cosmetics and household cleaners. Some more things to lock away: Vitamins (an overdose of iron is a toxin), mouthwash (it contains alcohol) and analgesic creams such as Ben-Gay (they contain methyl salicylate, which is twice as toxic as aspirin).
- Use non-breakable plastic cups, toothpaste holder, and soap dish.

1. Are hair dryers, shavers, curling irons and other appliances unplugged when not in use?

2. Are small appliances kept away from the sink or tub, and radios not allowed in bathrooms, to avoid electrical shocks?

3. Do tubs and shower floors have non-slippery surfaces?

4. Are cleaning agents stored out of reach of children and away from medications?

5. Are all prescriptions and over-the-counter medicines stored in their original containers, labeled, and out of the reach of children?

6. Are all medicines in one safe place, not left at the bedside, kitchen or in a purse where children can find them?

7. Do you regularly check to see if any medicines have passed their expiration date?

8. Before taking any medicine or giving it to another person, do family members read the label to be sure they are using the drug correctly?

Child's Room
- Move your child to a regular bed as soon as she is able to climb even partway up the side of her crib.

- Bed railings are intended for kids who can get out of bed on their own—typically two-to five-year-olds. If you do use a bed railing, make sure it has no gaps between three and a half and nine inches wide and no protruding screws or rivets.

- Keep drawers firmly shut so your child can't climb on them or catch her finger in them.

- Anchor chests and bookcases to the wall with a tether strap so they can't be tipped over.

- Arrange furniture to give you a clear path in and out of the room at night.

- Get a child-finder decal from your local fire department. Post it in the bedroom window so the fire department will know where to look in case of emergency.

- Use flame-retardant curtains. Avoid blinds or shades with pull-strings. If you do use blinds, tie the cords up high so they're out of reach.

- Use only cool-mist vaporizers — hot-mist ones can scald if a child gets too close.

- If any family members smoke, are ashtrays and smoking materials kept away from the bed? Is there a strict rule to NOT SMOKE in bed, or when liable to nap in a chair?

- Are electric blankets used as the top cover? (Never tuck them in to bend the wires. Also, nothing, including pets, should be on top of an electric blanket when it is in use).

Basements, Attics, Garages and Workshops
- Test your automated garage door by placing a cardboard box underneath it. If it can crush the box, it can crush your child too.

- Keep the garage floor free of spills.

- Keep all power equipment covered or out of reach.

- Tether all garage shelves so they can't topple over.

- Store all dangerous cleaners, chemicals and other products in locked cabinets.

1. Are these areas well lighted when in use, and can a light be turned on without walking through a dark or cluttered area?

2. Are gasolines, paint and other flammable liquids stored away from living areas, labeled, in tightly capped containers?

3. Are liquids that give off flammable vapors stored at considerable distance from ignition sources? (Gasoline within 10 feet of a water heater can explode.)

4. Are old magazine and newspapers thrown away regularly?

5. Are pesticides, flammable liquids and power tools out of reach of children, or locked up?

6. Is a working fire extinguisher handy?

Basements

- Never leave your child unattended.

- Make sure outdoor play equipment is safe, well constructed and positioned at least eight feet from fences or walls.

- All pools should be fenced with child-resistant spring lock gates and monitored with a water-activated pool alarm.

- Never use a power mower or other outdoor power equipment near a child; it can throw out loose rocks and other debris.

- Keep your child off balconies.

- Are the sidewalk and steps even and in good repair?

- Is the trash put in containers so those neighborhood animals cannot tear into it and spread it around?

- Are children's toys and bicycles put away when they are finished playing with them?

One third of all serious accidents occur at home, and children are especially at risk. The most frequent involve falls, fires, and misuse of home products or medications. Ninety percent of all accidents could be avoided if you follow simple safety rules and takes time to "accident proof" your home.

Prepare for Emergencies

1. Are there properly working smoke detectors in the hallways outside the kitchen and bedroom areas?

2. Are the smoke detectors checked periodically to make sure they are still working and batteries replaced when necessary?

3. Are emergency fire, ambulance, police and poison control numbers posted in large print next to each telephone in the house?

4. Is there an emergency exit plan for each room in the house in case of fire?

Examine Electrical cords and Outlets

1. Do outlets and switches have cover plates so that no wiring is exposed?

2. Are cords to appliances and fixtures in good condition or are they frayed or cracked and need to be replaced?

3. Are unused outlets covered?

4. Can you eliminate extension cords and move appliances closer to outlets?

5. Are there too many appliances on one outlet, which can overload the circuit and cause a fire? Unplug appliances when not in use..

You may find other hazards in and around your home that could seriously harm you or your children. It's best to take a look around frequently and get rid of these bad areas before something tragic occurs.

Places I must check:

_____

_____

_____

_____

_____

_____

Fire Safety Tips for the Home

A home fire can be the most devastating tragedy and is one of the most common causes of deaths in families. It is your responsibility to plan and take precautions to avoid such a suffering for you and your children. You need to discuss and make a fire plan and practice it frequently with your children.

- Install smoke detectors outside each sleeping area and on each floor of your home.
- Use the test button to check each smoke detector once a month. Replace the batteries twice a year to insure working condition. Replace the smoke detectors every 5 years.
- Have a good fire extinguisher in the kitchen and make sure it is properly charged.
- You can contact your local fire department on how to use the fire extinguisher if needed.
- Keep blankets, clothing, curtains, furniture and anything that could get hot and catch fire away from portable heaters. Follow all guidelines with portable heaters.
- Plug heaters directly into the wall socket and unplug them when they are not in use.
- Use safety plugs in electrical outlets, especially if you have small children.
- Avoid overloading electrical outlets and running cords under carpet and furniture.

Plan your escape route in case of fire:

- Draw a floor plan of your home and decide on at least two ways to escape from every room in the house.
- If you need an escape ladder, be certain everyone knows how to use it.
- Choose a location outside your home where everyone would meet after escaping.
- Practice your escape plan at least twice a year.
- Once you are out of a house on fire, Stay Out!
- Know how to call for emergency assistance.

Escape a burning building safely:

- If you see smoke in your first escape route, use your second way out. If you must exit through smoke, crawl under the smoke to escape.
- If you come to a closed door, feel the door before opening it. If it is HOT, use another route.
- If smoke, heat or flames block your exit route, stay in the room with the door closed. Signal for help using a bright-colored cloth at the window. If there is a telephone in the room, call the fire department and tell them where you are.

We can hope a fire never happens to you, but now you are prepared if it does!

Repair or Replace?

When you have purchased a product, you assume that you will get many years of service from it. However, things do break down. Many things are made of plastic today, and while they can last with good care, they can be expensive to repair and the replacement parts may be hard to find. Before you head to the store or the repair shop, check the troubleshooting guide in your owner's manual. You might call the manufacturer for help in getting the product to work also. You will need to establish the symptoms. What is not working? What have you tried? You then need to check on warranty coverage. If a warranty is in effect, your choice of repair shops may be limited to those the manufacturer will accept. And, a do-it-yourself repair may void the warranty coverage. If you don't have the sales receipt for an item under warranty, call the manufacturer to confirm your coverage. The manufacturer may offer to fix or replace the item at no charge, sometimes as part of a program to quietly appease customers of a trouble-prone model. If you decide to repair it, you will need to take the product to a shop that can fix it. All warranty repairs must be done at a manufacturer affiliated repair shop. Factory service facilities are owned by the manufacturer. Authorized service shops are privately run businesses having a contract agreement with the manufacturer. There are independent repair shops, which are usually safe for routine maintenance and minor repairs too. Ask questions like: Will repair labor be a flat fee or charged by the hour? When will the work be completed? If there is a warranty, does it cover parts, labor or both? Are there charges for just estimating the cost of repair? If you get an estimate, ask also that no repair work begin without your authorization. You may want to get a second or third estimate from other shops if the repair will be expensive. Remember that the cheapest is not necessarily the best.

Once you agree to have the work done, demand a detailed listing of the services performed, parts installed and warranties on the work. If you leave the item at the shop, ask for a dated claim check listing the brand, model and serial number, plus a promised completion date.

If you have a problem, see the section in this book on consumer complaints.

Things to have repaired: **Estimated cost**

_____

_____

_____

Things to have replaced: **Estimated cost**

_____

_____

_____

Home Maintenance Checks

The importance of making periodic home maintenance checks is to avoid a crisis, which could be very expensive, as well as disruptive, to your family. Whether you rent or own your home, you need to maintain a checklist and to see that necessary repairs are made before something dreadful happens. If you are renting, be certain that your landlord gets a copy of the needed repairs and make a note that you have provided this, in case it is needed in court.

- When you move into a home, you must know where important services are found which enter the home.
- Gas shut-off valve—Identify location and show the entire family how to shut off in case of a gas leak.
- Breaker box—Identify location and show entire family how to shut off main breaker.
- Water shut-off valve—Identify location and show entire family how to shut off the water in case of pipe breaks.
- Smoke detectors—Locate all appliances and be certain they are fully functional and properly located.

Every Month:
- Fire Extinguisher—Check that it is fully charged and recharge it if necessary. Be sure you have an adequate number located in the kitchen, garage and basement.
- Smoke detector—Clean the battery or indicator light.
- Sink and tub stoppers—Clean hair and soap residue out and flush with hot water.
- Breaker box—Trip circuit breakers and ground fault interrupters to insure proper protection.

Every Two Months:
- Wall furnace—Clean the grills. Clean or replace filter.
- Range hood fan—Clean grease filter.

Every Three Months:
- Faucets—Clean aerator by unscrewing and disassembling and washing out debris.
- Tub drain assembly—Clean out debris and scrub with baking soda.
- Dishwasher—Clean strainer, spray arm and air gap.

Every Six Months:
- Basement and foundation—Check foundation walls, floors, concrete and masonry for cracks, heaving or deterioration and moisture. Remove mold and mildew.
- Toilet—Check for leaks in the water feed, tank bottom and clean out mineral build-up.
- Interior caulking and grout—Inspect caulking and grout around tubs, showers and sinks. Thoroughly clean and remove mold and mildew and mineral build-up.
- Water Heater—Drain water until clear of sediment. Inspect flue assembly (gas heater); check for leaks and corrosion.
- Clothes washer—Clean water inlet filters, check hoses and replace if necessary.
- Clothes dryer—Vacuum lint from ducts and surrounding areas.
- Refrigerator—Clean drain hole and pan, wash door gasket, vacuum condenser coils to remove dust.
- Electrical wiring—Check for frayed cords and wires. Check exposed wiring in basement and get immediate repairs if necessary.
- Exhaust fans—Clean grill and fan blades.
- Bathroom—Check for leaks around and under sinks, showers, toilets and tubs.

Spring Maintenance

- Roof—Inspect roof surface flashing, eaves, and soffits, repair if necessary.
- Chimney/ stovepipe—Clean flue; repair any cracks in flue or any loose or crumbling mortar; check gasket on woodstove, and replace if necessary.
- Gutters and downspouts—Clean out; inspect and repair weaknesses; check for proper drainage and repair if necessary.
- Flashing—Check flashing around all surface projections and sidewalls.
- Siding and trim—Inspect and clean siding; Check all wood surfaces for weathering and paint failure; repair if necessary. Check joints between wood and masonry.
- Deck and porches—Check all decks, patios, porches, stairs and railings for loose members and deterioration.
- Exterior caulking—Inspect caulking and replace if deteriorating.
- Windowsills, doorsills and thresholds – Fill cracks, caulk edges, repaint; replace if necessary.
- Window and door screens—Clean screening and repair or replace if necessary; tighten or repair any loose or damaged frames and repaint if necessary; replace broken, worn, or missing hardware; tighten and lubricate door hinges and closers.
- Plumbing drain-waste and vent system   Flush out system.
- Hot-water heating systems—Lubricate circulating pump and motor.
- Evaporative air conditioner—Clean unit; check belt tension and adjust if necessary; replace cracked or worn belt.
- Antenna—Check antenna and satellite dish supports for possible leaks or breaks.
- Landscape—Cut back and trim all vegetation and overgrown bushes from being too close to the house, interfering with electrical lines, or other obstructions.

Fall Maintenance

- Storm windows and doors—Replace any cracked or broken glass, tighten or repair any loose or damaged frames and repaint if necessary; replace broken, worn, or missing hardware; tighten and lubricate door hinges and closers; check for broken or missing glazing.
- Window and door weather stripping—Inspect and repair or replace if deteriorating or missing.
- Forced warm-air heating system—Vacuum heat exchanger surfaces; clean and lubricate blower blades and motor; check fan belt tension and adjust if necessary; replace cracked or worn belt, check for leaks and repair if necessary.
- Gas burner—Clean burners and ports.
- Oil burner—Lubricate fan and motor bearings. Have professionally serviced.
- Thermostat—Clean heat sensor, contact points and contacts; check accuracy and replace if necessary.
- Garage doors—Clean and lubricate hinges, rollers and tracks; tighten screws.

Every Two Years:
- Carbon monoxide detector—change the sensor element.
- Septic tank—Have the septic tank cleaned and pumped.
- Water well—consider having well water tested for safety

Housecleaning

Why Clean?

1. You clean for space. We all need to feel free of physical and emotional crowded conditions.
2. Clean helps create control and management skills.
3. Clean creates sanitary and healthy environment. Who wants to be sick?
4. Clean for safety's sake. Accidents do happen.
5. Clean helps our stuff last longer, without costly repairs.
6. Clean keeps our environment better.
7. Clean to prevent waste.
8. Clean is more beautiful and serene
9. Clean gives others an impression of you.
10. Clean so that others will follow your example.

You have the responsibility to maintain your home to provide an appropriate growth environment for your children.

Daily Housekeeping Chores

1. Wash the dishes with soap and hot water after every meal
2. Make the beds
3. Pick up toys and clutter
4. Sweep or vacuum the floors
5. Clean the bathroom –scrub the sink, toilet and tub
6. Wash the dirty clothes
7. Put clean dishes and pots and pans away
8. Wash off kitchen counter and clean sink
9. Take one area to concentrate on for special organization
10. Empty wastebaskets into trash container

Weekly Housekeeping Chores

1. Do other laundry. Fold clothes or hang up in closet
2. Clean out refrigerator with soap and water, take care of food
3. Clean the stovetop with soap and water and wipe out oven of spilled food
4. Mop the floors, using soap and water, wax if you wish
5. Make the beds up with clean sheets
6. Wipe off furniture, tables and chairs, pick up toys and put away
7. Clean up yard of all trash and clutter
8. Clean out recycle bins and take to recycle center
9. Go over grocery list for shopping and set up menus for next week
10. Go over your time management schedule for appointments and other important dates

Here are some ideas on organizing your home

Bedroom Closet: If you organize your closets, you will find the clothes stay cleaner. Place the clothing that you wear most often within easy reach. Separate the long clothes from the short. Hang clothes like shirts and skirts by putting in both a low bar and a high bar. Adjustable poles set in the children's closet can be raised as they grow. Rotate seasonal clothing and store unused clothing in another closet. Put accessories that go with only one outfit in a plastic bag and fasten on the hanger with the clothing. Every six months go through the closet and remove clothes that do not fit, are outdated or otherwise unwearable and donate or dispose of these items. Put empty hangers on one end of the pole, so it is easy to find a hanger when hanging clothes back. Hang a bag on the closet for fine washables, so you can see when it is full, it is time to wash them all at once.

Utility Closet: Throw out old mops, sponges and broken-down brooms. Put cleaning supplies into a bucket, so that you have it ready when you clean. You can store small brushes or other supplies in an old shoe bag on the back of the door. Label the attachments to the vacuum cleaner so that anyone doing the job is sure to use the right parts. Put a flashlight and radio with batteries where everyone can find them in an emergency.

Kitchen Pantry: Post a grocery list inside the pantry door so that family members can add to it as you run out of items. Keep a large envelope next to the list for all coupons that you will be using when you go to the store. Place all cooking supplies grouped together that are used together, like baking goods, cake decorating and cookie supplies, meat grinders, etc. Place small packets of seasonings, sauces, gelatins or other condiments in a basket to find easily. You can place the spices according to height, or alphabetize them.

Linen Closet: You can fold towels and sheets, or you can roll them and stack them. Fold all the sheets and pillowcases that are part of a set into a pillowcase. You will have to grab only one item when making the bed. Items placed vertically, like books, are easier to take out and put back without spilling the whole pile. You can color-code the linens for each child, so they know which set belongs to them.

You can stack color-coded bins for each child to put mittens, hats, scarves, etc. You can put a hook inside the door for the house/car keys, if this is the place you always get your coat. Use hooks against the back wall for small children to hang up their coats.

Family Coat Closet: You can get your family to help out. Make a chore chart that is fair and easy to understand at a family meeting. Be sure your child has a chore that is age-appropriate. You can also give them a choice: dishes or trash, for example. The job is more likely to be done when it is a free choice. Be sure to set a time limit on when the job needs to be finished so you will not have to nag. Then, remember to appreciate the efforts. When all family members are invested into keeping the home organized, it is a happier place to be for everyone.

Videocassette Registry

Tape #	Video Title	Type of Movie (Comedy, drama)	Running Time
_____	_____	_____	_____ mins
_____	_____	_____	_____ mins
_____	_____	_____	_____ mins
_____	_____	_____	_____ mins
_____	_____	_____	_____ mins
_____	_____	_____	_____ mins
_____	_____	_____	_____ mins
_____	_____	_____	_____ mins
_____	_____	_____	_____ mins
_____	_____	_____	_____ mins
_____	_____	_____	_____ mins
_____	_____	_____	_____ mins
_____	_____	_____	_____ mins
_____	_____	_____	_____ mins
_____	_____	_____	_____ mins
_____	_____	_____	_____ mins
_____	_____	_____	_____ mins
_____	_____	_____	_____ mins
_____	_____	_____	_____ mins

Major Purchases Inventory

Item Purchased: _____   Date Purchased: _____

Serial Number: _____   Model Number: _____

Store purchased in: _____

Cost: $ _____   Payment method_____

Terms of Guarantee/Warranty _____

For Service Call: _____

Address: _____   Phone:_____

Additional Information: _____
_____

Item Purchased: _____   Date Purchased: _____

Serial Number: _____   Model Number: _____

Store purchased in: _____

Cost: $ _____   Payment method_____

Terms of Guarantee/Warranty _____

For Service Call: _____

Address: _____   Phone:_____

Additional Information: _____
_____

Item Purchased: _____   Date Purchased: _____

Serial Number: _____   Model Number: _____

Store purchased in: _____

Cost: $ _____   Payment method_____

Terms of Guarantee/Warranty _____

For Service Call: _____

Address: _____   Phone:_____

Additional Information: _____
_____

Major Purchases Inventory

Item Purchased: _____   Date Purchased: _____

Serial Number: _____   Model Number: _____

Store purchased in: _____

Cost: $ _____   Payment method_____

Terms of Guarantee/Warranty _____

For Service Call: _____

Address: _____   Phone:_____

Additional Information: _____
_____

Item Purchased: _____   Date Purchased: _____

Serial Number: _____   Model Number: _____

Store purchased in: _____

Cost: $ _____   Payment method_____

Terms of Guarantee/Warranty _____

For Service Call: _____

Address: _____   Phone:_____

Additional Information: _____
_____

Item Purchased: _____   Date Purchased: _____

Serial Number: _____   Model Number: _____

Store purchased in: _____

Cost: $ _____   Payment method_____

Terms of Guarantee/Warranty _____

For Service Call: _____

Address: _____   Phone:_____

Additional Information: _____
_____

My Chore Chart

Place a check in the boxes to the right for completed jobs.

		S	M	T	W	Th	F	S	good job!
My Room	Pick up all my toys/personal belongings								
	Clean my room								
	Make my bed								
Me	Brush my teeth (put toothpaste away)								
	Take a bath								
	Clean my ears								
	Clean my fingernails and toenails								
	Hang up towels and washcloth after bath								
My Clothes	Hang up all clothes (and coats)								
	Put all dirty clothes in the laundry								
	Fold clean clothes and put them away								
My Home	Take out trash and return trash cans								
	Vacuum and dust								
	Put my bike and skates away								
Meals	Wash my face and hands								
	Set the table/clear the table								
	Wash the dirty dishes								
	Clean up my mess after snacks								
School	Complete all my homework assignments								
	Make my lunch (or have lunch money ready)								
	Give notes from school to Mom or Dad								
	Keep track of all library books								
My Pets	Feed all pets (and don't forget fresh water)								
	Clean out cages and cat litter								
	Take dog out for exercise								
	Brush out fur								
Special Activities _____									
_____									

All jobs are to be completed by _____o'clock   Daily Totals: _____

Reward earned: _____

My Chore Chart

Place a check in the boxes to the right for completed jobs.

		S	M	T	W	Th	F	S	good job!
My Room	Pick up all my toys/personal belongings								
	Clean my room								
	Make my bed								
Me	Brush my teeth (put toothpaste away)								
	Take a bath								
	Clean my ears								
	Clean my fingernails and toenails								
	Hang up towels and washcloth after bath								
My Clothes	Hang up all clothes (and coats)								
	Put all dirty clothes in the laundry								
	Fold clean clothes and put them away								
My Home	Take out trash and return trash cans								
	Vacuum and dust								
	Put my bike and skates away								
Meals	Wash my face and hands								
	Set the table/clear the table								
	Wash the dirty dishes								
	Clean up my mess after snacks								
School	Complete all my homework assignments								
	Make my lunch (or have lunch money ready)								
	Give notes from school to Mom or Dad								
	Keep track of all library books								
My Pets	Feed all pets (and don't forget fresh water)								
	Clean out cages and cat litter								
	Take dog out for exercise								
	Brush out fur								

Special Activities _____

_____

_____

All jobs are to be completed by _____ o'clock

Daily Totals: _____

Reward earned: _____

Planning Your Family's Food and Nutrition

SECTION

8

Planning Your Family's Food and Nutrition

Your groceries will most likely be one of the costliest items in your budget. It is very wise to know how to shop and also feed your family well. We can be taken in by the marketing ploys used on us, so that we spend more money than we had planned to spend in the store. Grocery stores are planned to control your movement and decisions the minute you walk into the store. They want to sell you as much as possible so they can make a larger profit. You need to be aware of the food boutiques. These are the specialty cheese shops, the in-store bakery, the full-service fish market, the custom butcher, the gourmet food takeout and the candy boutiques. The food looks delicious, but remember that you will be paying extra for all the preparation. You might save by preparing the ingredients yourself and have fun doing it. The store is designed to make you slow down and zigzag through the produce section. There are colorful display units placed in these traffic hot spots to tempt you to buy. Do you know that the store also places the big name brands right at eye level and their brand below? They make more profit when you buy their brands and they attract you with the big names. If you are an impulse shopper, watch out for the end aisle displays and the floor stacks. People also tend to buy the products that they can sample in the store. The special sales may not be the best price, but when they are displayed in a colorful manner, with the music playing in the background, you are tempted to buy the products. The checkout scanners can also track your purchases every time you shop, especially when you sign up for a valued customer card.

The trick to grocery shopping is to have a list made out of the items you need. You want to get through the store in one pass. You will be in trouble if you have to double back for something. Even if you just have to run in for milk and bread, you will have to go to the back of the store, and pass by all the extras on the way. If you organize your list according to the layout of the store, you will be able to go down each aisle once. It helps to shop when the store is not busy, early in the morning.

Now, make your grocery list; check off items as you put them in your cart. Before you go to the checkout counter, count all the items in your cart and all the items on your list. Do the numbers match? Are there any extras? How much money extra? Gotcha!!

Safe Food

If you have ever been sick with food poisoning, you will never want to repeat that experience again! Children and the elderly are very vulnerable, as the dehydration can be fatal to them, as well as persons with a chronic illness. The safety of the food begins when you get the groceries from the store. Bring an ice chest if the time from the store to home will be longer than 30 minutes. Even short stops during hot summer weather may be enough to let the food warm up to unsafe temperatures and begin the growth of unsafe bacteria.

At the Grocery Store:
* Shop for meat, poultry and seafood last, and place them in plastic bags when possible to keep the blood and juice from dripping on other foods in your cart.
* Buy products that are labeled "keep refrigerated" only if they are stored in a refrigerated case and they are cold to the touch.
* Feel frozen foods to make sure they are rock solid.
* Choose canned goods that are free of dents, cracks, rust or bulging lids. Check packages for holes, tears and open corners.
* Purchase dated packages only if the "sell by" date has not expired.

In the Kitchen:
* Use a refrigerator thermometer to check that your refrigerator is cooling at 35°F to 40°F, and your freezer should be at 0°F or below.
* Space items in your refrigerator and freezer so air can circulate.
* Freeze fresh meat, poultry and fish immediately if you don't plan to use them within a couple of days. Overwrap packages with aluminum foil or heavy freezer wrap to make airtight.
* Wrap raw meat, poultry and fish, or place in separate plastic bags and set on the lowest shelf in the refrigerator to keep the blood and juices from dripping on other foods.
* Follow the "use by" or "keep refrigerated" and "safe handling" information on the package labels. If you can't remember when a food item was placed in the refrigerator, throw it out.

Before you Cook:
* Wash your hands with hot soapy water for at least 20 seconds before starting any food preparation. If you stop to do something else, be sure to wash your hands before touching the food again.
* Cover any cuts or sores on your hands with bandages, or use plastic gloves, to protect you and the food.
* Keep everything that touches food clean. Harmful bacteria can be found in many ways: dirty utensils, sponges or dishrags, and on plates or cutting boards.
* Keep raw meat, poultry, fish and their juices from any contact with other foods during preparation, especially food that won't be cooked. Wash your hands and all utensils and surfaces with hot, soapy water after they come in contact with raw meat.
* Never chop fresh vegetables or salad ingredients on a cutting board that was used for raw meat without properly cleaning it.
* Thaw foods only in the refrigerator or microwave oven, never leave it out at room temperature.
* Use a covered, non-metallic container to marinate meat. Place it in the refrigerator, not on the counter. Discard the leftover marinade that was in contact with the raw meat, or bring it to a rolling boil for one minute before using on cooked meat.
* Rinse thoroughly poultry and seafood in cold water and check for any off odors before cooking.
* Wash all fruits and vegetables with cold, running water, using a scrub brush if necessary.

Cooking Thoroughly:

- Cook eggs until the yolk and white are firm, not runny.
- Do not eat raw cookie dough or taste any meat or egg dish while it's raw or partially cooked.
- Roast meat or poultry in an oven temperature of 325∞F or above.
- Never partially heat foods and then refrigerate or set aside to finish cooking later. Partially cooked foods may not reach a high enough temperature to destroy bacteria.

Cooking Thoroughly:

- When basting grilled meats, brush sauce on the cooked surfaces only.
- Always place cooked foods in a clean dish for serving and use clean utensils. Never use the same unwashed plate that held raw meat.
- Do not allow any cooked food to sit out at room temperature for more than 2 hours.
- When serving from a buffet, keep cold foods on ice at a temperature below 40°F, and keep hot foods above 140°F until they are eaten. Do not mix fresh foods with food that's already been out for serving.

When You Travel Away:

- Carry food in insulated containers with a freeze pack or a small plastic bottle of frozen water. Keep food away from direct sunlight.
- Chill foods in the refrigerator before putting in the cooler.
- Never use leftover food that looks or smells strange to see if you can still use it. "When in doubt, throw it out."
- Dispose of unsafe food in a garbage disposal or a tightly wrapped package so that children or animals cannot eat it.

How to Freeze Food:

- Use fresh, quality food and freeze them as soon as possible. Cool hot food in the refrigerator before placing in the freezer.
- Store food in zip-top plastic freezer bags or rigid plastic containers, pressing out as much air as possible and store flat, or well wrapped in heavy-duty aluminum foil, freezer wrap or plastic wrap sealed with freezer tape.
- Label freezer bags and containers with food name, date frozen and portion size. You can color-code the labels to identify and date the packages.
- When stocking the freezer, put the new items in back and older ones in front, so you will use up the old stuff first. Arrange them so that you can easily read the labels without digging through everything. Keep small packages in one larger container so they don't get lost.
- Allow at least 1/2 inch space for expansion when freezing liquids.
- Trim meats of excess fat and debone large cuts if possible.
- Freeze hamburger patties, chops or cube steaks, wrapped double with plastic wrap for easy separation when frozen.
- Keep wrapped meats in freezer bags so you can remove what you need and reseal what remains.
- Fish should be cleaned, gutted, rinsed and dried.
- Do not season or marinate uncooked meats before freezing.

Foods that Don't Freeze Well:

- Cake and cookie icings made with egg whites.
- Cream fillings and soft frostings
- Custard or cream fillings in pies
- Cooked egg whites
- Cream cheese and other soft cheeses.
- Sour cream
- Potatoes in soups and stews.

After Thawing the Food:

Defrosting the food is very important to preserve the juiciness of meats, the texture and flavor of fruit and vegetables and moisture in baked goods. Defrost frozen food in the refrigerator overnight or in cold water, changing water every 30 minutes. To hasten thawing, immerse the sealed freezer bag or container in cold water, changing the water often. Transfer food to a microwave safe container and thaw on the defrost setting, then cook immediately.

Thaw bread, desserts and baked goods at room temperature in their original wrapping to avoid moisture loss.

How to Salvage Freezer Damage:

Gravy and fat-based sauces may separate—whisk or process them in a blender or food processor for a few minutes. Thickened sauces may need thinning—try water, milk, broth, or other to suit the dish. Seasonings, such as onions, herbs and spices used in dishes, may change flavor, Check and adjust the seasoning during reheating. Heavy whipping cream can be frozen if it's to be used for cooking, but it won't whip. Whipped cream can be frozen in dollops on a flat sheet. Once the dollops are solid, store them in zip top plastic freezer bags. Raw vegetables lose their crispness, but can be used for cooking soups and stews.

If the Food is:

Too salty. Add more liquid or solid ingredients to dilute the salty flavor. You may add more beans or vegetables to soup, or meat and vegetables to a stew. Potatoes are good to soak up extra salt. You can also try to mask the salty taste with a few pinches of brown sugar.

The soup is too thick or too thin. Thin soups by adding more water or broth. To thicken clear soups, mix 1 tablespoon of cornstarch with 2 tablespoons of water until smooth, then whisk into 2 quarts of simmering soup. Stir until it thickens. (Adding cornstarch directly into hot soup will clump up). You can also purée half the soup, then stir it back into the pot.

The bread is stale. To freshen bread, rolls or bagels, sprinkle with water and wrap in aluminum foil. Place in a 350-degree oven for about 10 minutes. You can crisp crackers in the oven on a baking sheet for about 5 minutes too.

Overcooked meat. If you have overcooked the roast, chicken or turkey, just make thin slices of the dry meat arranged on a plate and cover with gravy or sauce. You can turn meat that's stringy or falling apart into a goulash, stew stroganoff, or chili. Add it to stir-fried vegetables, or encase it in a tortilla with toppings.

The fish is too dry. Serve it with a citrus butter (warm butter with grated peel and a few spoonfuls of juice), a mustard vinaigrette with herbs and capers, or salsa. You can also serve the fish atop sautéed vegetables or salad. Or make fish cakes: mix flaked fish with eggs, bread crumbs, onion and seasonings, then form patties, dip them into bread crumb and sauté.

The vegetables are overdone. You can puree them, adding seasonings, butter, even Parmesan or ricotta cheese, and then serve like mashed potatoes. Or mix the puree with eggs, breadcrumbs, chopped onions and seasonings and pour into a greased pan and bake into a vegetable pudding.

The cake falls apart. Crumble the cake into a pan, layer on pudding or ice cream, fruit and whipped topping, and finish with nuts or candy pieces.

And remember all is never lost! Many great dishes have been found in mistakes! Be creative and enjoy!

Food Choices for Variety

(A Calorie Planner)

Fruits Choose 2-4

About 60 Calories per Serving:

1/2 Cup citrus or apple juice
3/4-1 cup berries
1 nectarine
1 peach
2 small tangerines
2 fresh apricots
1 small apple
1/2 banana
1/4 cantaloupe
1/8 honeydew melon
10 cherries
1 orange
2 medium plums
1/2 grapefruit
3 dates
1 medium kiwi fruit
1/2 large pear

Milk, Cheese

Adults choose 2
Teens (through age 24) choose 3
Pregnant moms choose 3
Breastfeeding moms choose 3

< calories per cup:

Skim milk
Low-fat/skim milk
Buttermilk
Dry curd cottage cheese
Nonfat dry milk
Evaporated skim milk

<120 calories per 1-1/2 oz.

Mozzarella cheese

<150 calories per 1/2 cup

Baked beans
Black-eyed peas
Chickpeas (garbanzos)
Lima beans
Kidney beans
White (Navy, Northern)

Vegetables Choose 3-5

Non-starchy vegetables: about 40 Calories per 1/2 cup cooked

Brussel sprouts
Carrots
String beans
Turnips
Rutabagas
Cauliflower
Cabbage
Broccoli
Okra
Beets
Celery
Mushrooms
Cucumbers
Artichoke
Greens
Green or red pepper
Lettuce
Eggplant
Onions
Radishes
Summer squash
Zucchini
Tomatoes
Asparagus
Bean sprouts

Fats, Sweets and Oils

(Use sparingly)

Bread, Cereal, Pasta Choose 6-11

About 80 Calories per serving

Bread (1 slice)
Crackers
1/2 hamburger bun
1/2 cup oatmeal or cooked cereal
1 tortilla
1 pancake (4 inch)
1/2 bagel, English Muffin
15 oyster crackers
1/2—3/4 cup ready-to-eat cereal
1/2 muffin
1/2 cup macaroni
1 small dinner roll
3 graham crackers

Meat, Poultry, Fish, Eggs

<165 Calories per 3-oz. serving

Poultry (no skin)
Fish (baked or broiled)
Lean beef roast (round)
Lean leg of lamb
Canned ham
Canadian bacon
Lean cured ham
Boiled ham
2 eggs
Turkey, chicken (light meat, no skin)
1 chicken or turkey frank
Clams, crab, shrimp, tuna (water)
Less than 150 calories:

Less than 150 calories:

1/2 cup custard, ice cream (10% fat)
1/2 cup sherbet
Angel food cake—1 slice
1 cupcake (1-1/2 inch across)
2 small cookies
2 fig bars
6 vanilla wafers
1/2 cup pudding (skim milk)
3/4 cup frozen yogurt
2 fruit bars or popsicles
15 potato or corn chips
5 cups air-popped popcorn
2-1/2 cups popcorn (popped in vegetable oil)
Ginger ale—8 oz.
4 caramels
15 jelly beans

Select a variety of foods every day, plan your meals, and shop wisely. Make the most of seasonal vegetables and fruits.

Grocery List

Bread, cereal, pasta

_____ _____ _____
_____ _____ _____
_____ _____ _____
_____ _____ _____
_____ _____ _____
_____

Meat, poultry, fish, eggs

_____ _____ _____
_____ _____ _____
_____ _____ _____
_____ _____ _____
_____ _____ _____

Vegetables

_____ _____ _____
_____ _____ _____
_____ _____ _____
_____ _____ _____
_____ _____ _____

Fruits

_____ _____ _____
_____ _____ _____
_____ _____ _____
_____ _____ _____
_____ _____ _____

Fats, sweets, oils

_____ _____ _____
_____ _____ _____
_____ _____ _____
_____ _____ _____
_____ _____ _____

	Day 1	Day 2	Day 3	Day 4	Day 5	Day 6	Day 7
Meal 1							
Meal 2							
Meal 3							
Snacks							

	Day 1	Day 2	Day 3	Day 4	Day 5	Day 6	Day 7
Fruits ☐☐ _ _	Fruits ☐☐ _ _	Fruits ☐☐ _ _	Fruits ☐☐ _ _	Fruits ☐☐ _ _	Fruits ☐☐ _ _	Fruits ☐☐ _ _
Vegetables ☐☐☐ _ _	Vegetables ☐☐☐ _ _	Vegetables ☐☐☐ _ _	Vegetables ☐☐☐ _ _	Vegetables ☐☐☐ _ _	Vegetables ☐☐☐ _ _	Vegetables ☐☐☐ _ _
Bread, cereal, pasta ☐☐☐☐☐ _ _ _ _ _	Bread, cereal, pasta ☐☐☐☐☐ _ _ _ _ _	Bread, cereal, pasta ☐☐☐☐☐ _ _ _ _ _	Bread, cereal, pasta ☐☐☐☐☐ _ _ _ _ _	Bread, cereal, pasta ☐☐☐☐☐ _ _ _ _ _	Bread, cereal, pasta ☐☐☐☐☐ _ _ _ _ _	Bread, cereal, pasta ☐☐☐☐☐ _ _ _ _ _
Dried Beans, Peas, Meat, Fish, Eggs ☐☐	Dried Beans, Peas, Meat, Fish, Eggs ☐☐	Dried Beans, Peas, Meat, Fish, Eggs ☐☐	Dried Beans, Peas, Meat, Fish, Eggs ☐☐	Dried Beans, Peas, Meat, Fish, Eggs ☐☐	Dried Beans, Peas, Meat, Fish, Eggs ☐☐	Dried Beans, Peas, Meat, Fish, Eggs ☐☐
Milk, cheese ☐☐	Milk, cheese ☐☐	Milk, cheese ☐☐	Milk, cheese ☐☐	Milk, cheese ☐☐	Milk, cheese ☐☐	Milk, cheese ☐☐
Other: _ _ _ _	Other: _ _ _ _	Other: _ _ _ _	Other: _ _ _ _	Other: _ _ _ _	Other: _ _ _ _	Other: _ _ _ _

Education/Employment

SECTION
9

My Educational Records

This section is a compilation of your education. It includes those experiences that you have had in a primary educational setting, like school. It also includes those experiences that you have had in which you added to your total knowledge of the world in which you live. When you have put together this information, you then have a chance to evaluate that learning for yourself. What did it do for you? Was it helpful, and if not, what happened that did not benefit you?

In this section, add those self-assessments that you have taken—like the DISC or the Values Profile, Interest Inventories, Creative Profiles, Aptitude and Achievement assessments, and Intelligence profiles. In this way, you can contrast and compare notes on yourself.

Every day you add to your total knowledge, even if you are unaware of it happening. This comes in many forms besides schooling. Each of us feels more comfortable in some studies than others. What is your pattern? Are there areas that you enjoyed but have forgotten to pursue? Are there some areas that you have always been afraid to look into? When you see where you have been, you can gain some insight into where you might go next. You may have to be your own teacher as well as student. Your education is part of your total life plan.

My Educational Record

Name of school	Address	I attended from - to	Certificates/Awards
Preschool			
First grade			
Second			
Third			
Fourth			
Fifth			
Sixth			
Seventh			
Eighth			

My best year in school was: _____

My worst year in school was: _____

Special activities I participated in during school: _____
_____
_____

Special activities I participated in outside of school: _____
_____
_____

My High School Record

Name of Student: _____

School(s) attended: _____ Dates from _____ to _____

Address: _____

attended: _____ Dates from _____ to _____

Address: _____

attended: _____ Dates from _____ to _____

Grades completed: _____

Graduation Date: _____

I belonged to:

Clubs/Activities: _____

_____

Sports: _____

_____

Honors/Awards: _____

_____

Trade groups/Practical skills: _____

_____

PSAT: Date taken: _____ Score received: _____

SAT: Date taken: _____ Score received: _____

Advanced Placement (AP) Courses:

Course: _____	Date Taken	AP Test grade	College Credit
_____	_____to_____	_____	_____
_____	_____to_____	_____	_____
_____	_____to_____	_____	_____
_____	_____to_____	_____	_____
_____	_____to_____	_____	_____
_____	_____to_____	_____	_____
_____	_____to_____	_____	_____

Evaluating My High School Years

Ninth Grade:

Classes	Teacher	My Final Grade	What I got out of it

My evaluation of the year: _____

Tenth Grade:

Classes	Teacher	My Final Grade	What I got out of it

My evaluation of the year: _____

Eleventh Grade:

Classes	Teacher	My Final Grade	What I got out of it

My evaluation of the year: _____

Twelfth Grade:

Classes	Teacher	My Final Grade	What I got out of it

My evaluation of the year: _____

My Educational Plan

What is my ultimate goal? _____

_____

_____

What would be the most effective and simplest way of reaching this goal? _____

_____

_____

What would be my rewards for reaching this goal? _____

_____

_____

How will attaining this goal fit in with my total life plan? _____

_____

_____

What would I need to get me started? _____

_____

_____

My First Step:

I have the following skills, knowledge and abilities to achieve this goal: _____

_____

_____

But I think I will need additional information, skills and abilities in: _____

_____

_____

Here are the places I will go, the people I will see, and the sources I will use to help me gain the new information, skills and abilities I need: _____

_____

_____

My target date for reaching this goal is: _____

My Educational Contract with Myself

I Can Do This!

Date: _____

To get myself started, I will: _____
_____this week.

My next main steps will be as follows:

To do: By Date:

1. _____   _____
   _____   _____

2. _____   _____
   _____   _____

3. _____   _____
   _____   _____

4. _____   _____
   _____   _____

5. _____   _____
   _____   _____

After accomplishing the above tasks, I will re-evaluate my position for
further progress. My deadline for doing this is (date) _____

I also think I will reward myself for getting this far by: _____
_____
_____

Yes, I Can Do This!

My Employment Records

This section is a compilation of your work experiences. This record includes those jobs that you had even as a child, such as a paper route, lawn work, babysitting, etc. This work was something that you were paid for. Include even the smallest jobs. The money your dad gave you for doing the dishes when your mom was sick is as important as any job you held as an adult. It is because there is a certain value to others as well as yourself in the work world. Why do you work? As you recall your work experiences, think about how you felt in doing that job. Did you feel competent at it? Did you do a good job? Were you satisfied with it? Or did you feel unprepared? Do not be afraid to look at your mistakes. Many mistakes are a key to success.

My Career Plan

What is my ultimate goal? _____

What would be the most effective and simplest way of reaching this goal? _____
_____
_____

What would be my rewards for reaching this goal?_____
_____
_____

How will attaining this goal fit in with my total life plan? _____
_____
_____
_____
_____

What would I need to get me started? _____

But I think I will need additional information, skills and abilities in: _____
_____

Here are the places I will go, the people I will see and the sources I will use to help me gain the new information, skills and abilities I need: _____
_____
_____
_____
_____

My Career Contract with Myself

My target date for reaching this goal is: _____

Date: _____

To get myself started, I will: _____
_____ this week.

My next main steps will be as follows:

To do: By Date:

1. _____   _____
   _____   _____

2. _____   _____
   _____   _____

3. _____   _____
   _____   _____

4. _____   _____
   _____   _____

5. _____   _____
   _____   _____

After accomplishing the above tasks, I will re-evaluate my position for further progress. My deadline for doing this is (date) _____

I think I should reward myself for getting this far by: _____
_____
_____

I Can Do This!

Volunteer Record

Name: _____

Place Volunteered: _____

Location: _____ Phone: _____

My Supervisor: _____

My Duties: _____

Dates Worked:

_____

_____

_____

_____

_____

_____

_____

_____

_____

_____

Hours Worked:

_____

_____

_____

_____

_____

_____

_____

_____

_____

_____

Total Hours Worked: _____

Comments:

_____

_____

_____

Volunteer Record

Name: _____

Place Volunteered: _____

Location: _____ Phone: _____

My Supervisor: _____

My Duties: _____

Dates Worked: Hours Worked:

_____   _____

_____   _____

_____   _____

_____   _____

_____   _____

_____   _____

_____   _____

_____   _____

_____   _____

_____   _____

_____   _____

                               Total Hours Worked: _____

Comments:

_____

_____

_____

Vocational/Professional Training Record

Name: _____

Name of School/Training Center: _____

Address: _____ Phone: _____

Company Sponsor (if applicable): _____

Purpose: _____

Skills/equipment learned: _____

Certificates/Awards received: _____

Name of School/Training Center: _____

Address: _____ Phone: _____

Company Sponsor (if applicable): _____

Purpose: _____

Skills/equipment learned: _____

Certificates/Awards received: _____

Name of School/Training Center: _____

Address: _____ Phone: _____

Company Sponsor (if applicable): _____

Purpose: _____

Skills/equipment learned: _____

Certificates/Awards received: _____

Name of School/Training Center: _____

Address: _____ Phone: _____

Company Sponsor (if applicable): _____

Purpose: _____

Skills/equipment learned: _____

Certificates/Awards received: _____

My Record of Service in the Armed Forces

Name: _____   Serial No.:_____

M.O.S. number: _____

Enlisted or inducted: _____   Date: _____

Place_____   Branch of Service:_____

Training: _____

Camps: _____   From: _____   To: _____

_____   _____   _____

Service Schools I attended: _____

Division: _____   Regiment: ____   Dept./Ship _____   Dates _____

_____   _____   _____   _____

_____   _____   _____   _____

Company: _____

Transferred: _____

Promotions: _____   on Date: _____

_____   _____

_____   _____

Overseas service: Depart _____   on Date: _____

Returned on: _____

Depart _____   on Date: _____

Returned on: _____

I saw action on: _____

_____

My commanding officers were: _____

_____

Citations I received: _____

Important leaves or furloughs: _____

Discharge/Separation at: _____   Grade: _____   Age _____

Reserve term: _____   Beg. Grade: _____   End grade: _____

Dates: _____

My Job History Record

Name: _____

Employer: _____
Address: _____
Type of Business/Organization: _____
My Title/Position:_____ Hrs./Week:_____
Dates Employed: From_____ to _____
Starting salary: $_____ Ending salary: $_____
My job responsibilities:_____
Name of supervisor: _____
Reason for leaving: _____
Comments: _____
_____

Employer: _____
Address: _____
Type of Business/Organization: _____
My Title/Position:_____ Hrs./Week:_____
Dates Employed: From_____ to _____
Starting salary: $_____ Ending salary: $_____
My job responsibilities:_____
Name of supervisor: _____
Reason for leaving: _____
Comments: _____
_____

Employer: _____
Address: _____
Type of Business/Organization: _____
My Title/Position:_____ Hrs./Week:_____
Dates Employed: From_____ to _____
Starting salary: $_____ Ending salary: $_____
My job responsibilities:_____
Name of supervisor: _____
Reason for leaving: _____
Comments: _____
_____

Finding a Job

The good thing about education is that you also learn not to be "taken in" by fraudulent scams or con artists. So, getting as much education as you can get will help you understand a little bit about a lot of things so that you can ask intelligent questions.

Unfortunately, there has not been much of a bridge between school years and work years unless you know where you are going. If you know what you want to do and you have set the goals to get there, you will not be casting about in a quandary. However, if you do not know what you want to do and have no idea how to start out, then here are ideas to help you.

1. What interests you? Think of special abilities and skills you already have. You can develop creativity and expertise in areas of personal interest. Join clubs or take classes in areas that interest you. You will meet new people and find out where possible jobs are located. Let people know you are looking for work.

2. You can volunteer. Volunteering is an excellent way to meet people and find a niche that may work out for you. There are many agencies and non-profit organizations that are badly in need of help. Even if you just sweep the floors, you will get to know the people there. They can help you.

3. Always grow personally. In the process of learning new skills, gaining new insights and achieving a sense of accomplishment you will build your self-confidence and ability to handle more job transference.

4. Keep records of your education and experience to draw from when you need to produce a résumé or market yourself.

5. Discuss with a friend the worst job you ever had—what was bad about it?

6. Discuss with a friend the best job you ever had—what was good about it?

7. Write down five things that are pretty important to you in any job you take:_____

_____

_____

_____

_____

_____

_____

_____

Job Hunting Tips

Cover Letters:

Specify which job you're applying for and how you found out about it. Many employers prefer typed cover letters. Watch out for grammatical errors and spelling goofs, especially in names. Keep it short and professional. Each letter should be addressed by name to the person you want to talk with. That person is the one who can hire you. It will most likely be the person who will supervise you once you start work.

Cover letters are sales letters. Start by talking about the company and mention current projects you know about or favorable comments recently published about the company. You can find this information in the business section of the local newspaper. If you are answering an ad, mention it. The body of your letter then gives a brief description of your qualifications and refers to the résumé. At the end of the letter, request an interview. Suggest a time and say that you will call to confirm the appointment. Use a standard complimentary close, such as "Sincerely yours," leaving three or four lines for your signature, and type your name, address and phone number.

Résumés:

This often is an employer's first impression of you. Do some homework on effective résumé writing, or hire the job done. A poorly designed or badly written résumé will quickly close doors. Experts suggest using bullets or other design elements to help potential employers quickly assess your abilities and experience. Use white paper, unless applying for jobs in creative or artistic fields, and keep the length down to two pages or less.

Effective Résumés include:

- Current address and phone number. If you are rarely at home, be sure to give the phone number of a friend or relative that knows where you can be reached.

- Job you are seeking or your career goal.

- Experience (both paid and volunteer) dates of employment, name and full address of the employer, job title, starting and finishing salary, and reason for leaving (moving, returning to school, and seeking a better position are accepted reasons).

- Education – the school's name, the city in which it is located, the years you attended it, the diploma or certificate you earned, and the course of studies you pursued.

- Other qualifications—your hobbies, organizations you belong to, honors you have received and leadership positions you have held.

- Office machines, tools, and equipment you have used and skills that you possess. Your competency on computers is important, too.

Homework before the Interview:
Study up on your employer and the requirements of the job. List some questions about the position that you will ask during the interview, including exact job duties, salary and other benefits. Practice potential interview questions about career goals, your qualifications and why you want that job with that company.

The Interview:
Dress to impress. If in doubt, dress up rather than down to show you take the interview seriously. Plan ahead to bring needed materials and show up early, calm and collected. Shake hands and make eye contact. You may want to practice answering possible questions with a friend before your interview appointment. Here is a list of some commonly asked questions:

- Why did you apply for this job?
- Why did you choose this career?
- What do you know about this job or company?
- Why should I hire you?
- What would you do if.....
- How would you describe yourself?
- What would you like to tell me about yourself?
- What are your major strengths?
- What are your major weaknesses?
- What type of work do you like to do best?
- What are your interests outside work?
- What type of work do you like to do least?
- What accomplishment gave you the greatest satisfaction?
- What was your worst mistake?
- What would you change in your past life?
- What courses did you like best or least in school?
- What did you like best or least about your last job?
- Why did you leave your last job?
- Why were you fired?
- How does your education or experience relate to this job?
- What are your goals?
- How do you plan to reach them?
- What do you hope to be doing in five years? In ten years?

Here are some questions you may want to ask the interviewer:
- What salary do you expect?
- What would a day on this job be like?

- Whom would I report to? May I meet this person?
- How important is this job to the company?
- What training programs are offered?
- What advancement opportunities are offered?
- Why did the last person leave this job?
- What is that person doing now?
- What is the greatest challenge of this position?
- What plans does the company have with regard to ......?
- Is the company growing?

Immediately after the interview, make notes of what went well and what you would like to improve. Then send a follow-up letter to the interviewer, thanking him/her for their consideration.

Following up: Try a follow-up phone call or letter. Do not, however, pester potential employers. Thank them again for their consideration. Good manners do matter!

Make a good First Impression!

It takes only 3 seconds to make a first impression—good or bad.

Head to toe checklist:

Hair: Neatness counts. Hair should be clean and off your face, looking natural. If you are going to try a new haircut, do it a week or two before your interview, to give you time to get used to it.

Skin: Your skin should be clean and any blotches or pimples can be treated and then camouflaged with concealer and foundation. Don't go overboard on makeup unless you are applying for a theatre job.

Hands and Feet: Hands and shoes are the two most telling nonverbal cues corporate recruiters look at. Nails should be short, polish neutral. Use lotion if hands are rough and chapped. Don't wear stiletto heels. Flats are too casual. One- or two-inch heels are professional. Stockings should match or coordinate with your outfit.

Clothes: Find out the dress code, if you can, where you're about to interview. It's best to err on the tailored, conservative side. What you might wear on the job might not be appropriate for getting that job. Wear something you feel comfortable in, a great skirt or dress with a terrific jacket, or a suit. No micro minis or anything shorter that seventeen inches.

What you look like speaks volumes, but what you say matters, too.

Speak like a grownup. Don't use slang or baby talk and don't whine or complain. When you are asked a difficult question, just say, "That's a good question. I need a moment to think."

Remember your manners. As you shake hands with the interviewer, say, " Thank you for meeting with me." Try to be as positive as you can. A cheerful manner gives a good impression. Listen to your own voice as you speak. Watch out for mumbling and try not to speak too fast. If you relax, you will appear more confident.

Contacts Made

Name of business contact: _____

Company: _____

Person's title: _____ Phone: _____

Met at: _____ Date : _____

Issues discussed: _____

Suggestions made : _____

_____

_____

Name of business contact: _____

Company: _____

Person's title: _____ Phone: _____

Met at: _____ Date : _____

Issues discussed: _____

Suggestions made : _____

_____

_____

Name of business contact: _____

Company: _____

Person's title: _____ Phone: _____

Met at: _____ Date : _____

Issues discussed: _____

Suggestions made : _____

_____

_____

Name of business contact: _____

Company: _____

Person's title: _____ Phone: _____

Met at: _____ Date : _____

Issues discussed: _____

Suggestions made : _____

_____

_____

Hourly Work Schedule

Name: _____

Employer: _____

Location: _____

Salary/Hour: $ _____

Hours Worked:

Week of:	Sun.	Mon.	Tue.	Wed.	Thu.	Fri.	Sat.	Total hrs.	Total Pay
____	____	____	____	____	____	____	____	____	____
____	____	____	____	____	____	____	____	____	____
____	____	____	____	____	____	____	____	____	____
____	____	____	____	____	____	____	____	____	____
____	____	____	____	____	____	____	____	____	____
____	____	____	____	____	____	____	____	____	____
____	____	____	____	____	____	____	____	____	____
____	____	____	____	____	____	____	____	____	____
____	____	____	____	____	____	____	____	____	____
____	____	____	____	____	____	____	____	____	____
____	____	____	____	____	____	____	____	____	____
____	____	____	____	____	____	____	____	____	____
____	____	____	____	____	____	____	____	____	____
____	____	____	____	____	____	____	____	____	____

Hourly Work Schedule

Name: _____

Employer: _____

Location: _____

Salary/Hour: $_____

Hours Worked:

Week of:	Sun.	Mon.	Tue.	Wed.	Thu.	Fri.	Sat.	Total hrs.	Total Pay
_____	____	____	____	____	____	____	____	____	____
_____	____	____	____	____	____	____	____	____	____
_____	____	____	____	____	____	____	____	____	____
_____	____	____	____	____	____	____	____	____	____
_____	____	____	____	____	____	____	____	____	____
_____	____	____	____	____	____	____	____	____	____
_____	____	____	____	____	____	____	____	____	____
_____	____	____	____	____	____	____	____	____	____
_____	____	____	____	____	____	____	____	____	____
_____	____	____	____	____	____	____	____	____	____
_____	____	____	____	____	____	____	____	____	____
_____	____	____	____	____	____	____	____	____	____
_____	____	____	____	____	____	____	____	____	____
_____	____	____	____	____	____	____	____	____	____

Specific Workshops or Training I have had for Each Job

Class _____ Dates _____

Location_____

Certification_____

Educational credits_____

Course materials_____

Tools needed _____

Benefits to the job _____

Personal benefits to me_____

Class _____ Dates _____

Location_____

Certification_____

Educational credits_____

Course materials_____

Tools needed _____

Benefits to the job _____

Personal benefits to me_____

Class _____ Dates _____

Location_____

Certification_____

Educational credits_____

Course materials_____

Tools needed _____

Benefits to the job _____

Personal benefits to me_____

Class _____ Dates _____

Location_____

Certification_____

Educational credits_____

Course materials_____

Tools needed _____

Benefits to the job _____

Personal benefits to me_____

Specific Workshops or Training I have had for Each Job

Class _____ Dates _____

Location_____

Certification_____

Educational credits_____

Course materials_____

Tools needed _____

Benefits to the job _____

Personal benefits to me_____

Class _____ Dates _____

Location_____

Certification_____

Educational credits_____

Course materials_____

Tools needed _____

Benefits to the job _____

Personal benefits to me_____

Class _____ Dates _____

Location_____

Certification_____

Educational credits_____

Course materials_____

Tools needed _____

Benefits to the job _____

Personal benefits to me_____

Class _____ Dates _____

Location_____

Certification_____

Educational credits_____

Course materials_____

Tools needed _____

Benefits to the job _____

Personal benefits to me_____

What to Do if You Lose Your Job

What happens after you lose a job will be your time to make choices. You may have many options to choose from. Some people choose to retire, some to change careers, some will go back to school full- or part-time, some may decide to start a business of their own. If you consider all your options, you can make a satisfactory choice that is right for you.

- **First, make a schedule.** A schedule helps plan the day and the week so that you know when you are going to spend time on your job search, when you are going to take care of other business and when you are going to relax. You make plans to take charge of your own life and its direction.

- **Gather Information.** Look into your skills inventory. You have experience now. What are your likes, dislikes, work values, priorities, skills and abilities? Find out about possible job opportunities in your local area that might have work you would be interested in.

- **Set some long-term and short-term goals.** Consider what needs to be done right away. You might want to work up a new résumé, investigate classes you might like to take, get some household chores done that you have not had the time to do while you were working. You also need to consider what long-term plans you may wish for further training and education or for a whole new career.

- **Network.** This means letting others know you are looking for work. Talk to your friends, family, neighbors and acquaintances and ask them to let you know if they find out about a job you would be interested in.

- **Be creative in looking for a job.** Don't just rely on want ads in the newspaper. There are many good jobs that have not been advertised. You can call and set up times to visit employers that you would like to work for, even if they don't have openings at the moment.

- **Prepare for job interviews.** You can practice and prepare for interviews. The more relaxed you feel at an interview, the more confident and self-assured you will appear. Think about and practice the questions you may be asked and those questions that you will ask yourself.

- **Be good to yourself.** Eating right, exercising and getting enough rest will help you physically maintain energy and enthusiasm, which will help you appear ready for a good job. Keep in touch with friends and former co-workers. Friendly support is always a foundation for self-esteem.

- **Review, Revise and Reward yourself.** As you look at your goals, frequently check to see that you are still headed for the destination where you want to go. Do you need to revise your plans? Is there any information you are lacking? Reward yourself as each level is reached. After all, you should know yourself best of all. Make it worth your while.

My Specific Plan for Employment

What do I really want to accomplish? _____
_____
_____

Target date for completion _____

What is the most effective and expedient means of reaching my goal? _____
_____
_____
_____

Target Date for Completion _____

My knowledge, skills and abilities to help me achieve this goal: _____
_____
_____

Here is the exact first step I will take this week. _____
_____
_____

Target date _____

Additional information, skills, and abilities I need: _____
_____

Target date: _____

My next main step: _____
_____

Target date: _____

Places, people, sources I will use to gain new information: _____
_____
_____

My next main step: _____
_____

Target date: _____

Yes, I can do this!

Planning for My Later Years

I plan to retire from work, but not from life, when I reach _____ years of age.

My total monthly income will be: $ _____

My total monthly expenses will be: $ _____

I will have $_____ in reserve for emergencies.

Where shall I live? (Name the state, city and location) _____

Will I have enough money to live on? _____

What will I be doing? _____

What about my health? _____

What are my plans? _____

Do I have a sound, up-to-date will made up? _____

Have I provided an experienced executor with investment and discretionary powers broad enough to pro-tect my family? _____

What information do I need to accumulate to help me plan for my retirement and with whom should I speak to obtain this information? _____

_____

_____

_____

Have I discussed my plans with other members of my family? _____

What are their plans? _____

_____

_____

_____

_____

_____

How to Find a Place to Live

SECTION
10

Housing Questions to Ask

1. Are you living where you desire to live? Ask yourself, "How do I live and what is important to me?"

Number of members in my family _____

	These are very important	These are least important
City life	_____	_____
Rural life	_____	_____
Close to my job	_____	_____
Close to my family	_____	_____
Close to my friends	_____	_____
Need transportation	_____	_____
Close to shopping	_____	_____
Close to my doctor	_____	_____
Hospital nearby	_____	_____
Need services near	_____	_____
(CMH, PHD, FIA)		
House with backyard	_____	_____
Small house	_____	_____
Studio apartment	_____	_____
Apartment with 1 bedroom	_____	_____
Need two bedrooms	_____	_____
Need three bedrooms	_____	_____
Need four or more bedrooms	_____	_____
Need appliances furnished	_____	_____
Need washing facilities	_____	_____
Need outside clothesline to dry	_____	_____
Need clothes dryer	_____	_____
Need cable TV	_____	_____
Need parking for car	_____	_____
Need garage or carport	_____	_____
Need space for a garden	_____	_____
Close to schools	_____	_____
Need telephone service	_____	_____
Need garbage pick up	_____	_____
Need internet service	_____	_____
Need playground nearby	_____	_____

Steps to Take

1. Obtain a housing list from FIA, or search newspapers for possible choices.
2. Call real-estate agents in the area for additional choices.
3. Make a list of the ones you want to check out.
4. Call the phone numbers listed with the ad and keep a list of the persons you talk to and what they have told you.
5. If it sounds like something you want, ask questions.
6. What area is it in? Street address and directions?_____
    _____
7. Is this a house or apartment? _____
8. What school district is it in? _____
9. Is it in town or out of town?_____
10. Landlord's name: _____
    address:_____ phone number: _____

What is the monthly rent? _____

Is there a security deposit required? _____

Are the utilities included in the rent? _____

How much does the heat and utilities run each month?   heat: _____

                                                       electric: _____

                                                       water:_____

Are pets allowed? Any size or weight limits? _____

Is garbage pick up included? _____

What is the cost for garbage pick-up?_____

When will the unit be available? _____

When can I look at it? _____

Who were the last renters? _____

Why did they leave?_____

If repairs need to be made, can it be deducted from the rent? _____

Do you need references? How many?_____

Are there housing codes that must be followed? _____

                                      Smoke detectors required? _____

                                      Recycling of waste required?_____

How is the neighborhood safety? Is the crime rate high? _____

Where are the playgrounds or parks? _____
_____

How long did the past resident stay? _____

Has building ever suffered a disaster, like flood or earthquake?_____

How many persons can occupy this unit? _____

How long can guests stay? _____

Contact List

Date	Home address	Landlord	Address	Phone

Inventory Checklist

You should complete this checklist, noting the condition of the rental property and return it to the landlord within 7 days after obtaining possession of the rental unit. You are also entitled to request and receive a copy of the last termination inventory checklist which shows what claims were chargeable to the prior tenants.

	Beginning Condition	Ending Condition
Living Room		
Door (including locks)		
Windows		
Carpet or floor		
Walls		
Ceiling		
Lights and switches		
Other:		
Dining Room		
Windows		
Carpet or floor		
Walls		
Ceiling		
Lights and switches		
Other:		
Hallway		
Floor		
Walls		
Ceiling		
Other:		
Other:		
Kitchen		
Windows		
Floor		
Walls		
Ceiling		
Lights and switches		
Stove		
Refrigerator		
Sink (hot and cold water)		
Cabinets and countertops		
Other:		
Bedroom		
Door		
Windows		
Walls		
Carpet or floor		
Ceiling		
Lights and switches		
Closet		
Other:		

Bathroom	**Beginning Condition**	**Ending Condition**
Door	_____	_____
Window	_____	_____
Floor	_____	_____
Walls	_____	_____
Ceiling	_____	_____
Sink (hot and cold water)	_____	_____
Tub and/or shower	_____	_____
Toilet	_____	_____
Cabinet, shelves, closet	_____	_____
Towel bars	_____	_____
Lights and switches	_____	_____
Other:	_____	_____

Furniture inventory
(use if unit is furnished, check condition of items and number present):

		Beginning Condition	**Ending Condition**
Kitchen chairs	number _____	_____	_____
Tables	_____	_____	_____
End tables	_____	_____	_____
Lounge chairs	_____	_____	_____
Sofas	_____	_____	_____
Lamps	_____	_____	_____
Desks	_____	_____	_____
Desk chairs	_____	_____	_____
Bookcases	_____	_____	_____
Beds and mattresses	_____	_____	_____
Dressers	_____	_____	_____

Address of unit: _____

_____

Signature of Landlord _____ Date: _____
Address: _____ Phone: _____

Signature of tenant _____ Date: _____

Landlord/Tenant Laws

It is best to have a written agreement that is signed by both parties in case of misunderstandings.

Provisions of the Rental Agreement

Leases differ in terms, but a written rental contract should include:

1. The names and signatures of the landlords.

2. The names and signatures of the tenants.

3. The amount of rent to be paid, how frequently, and when it is to be paid.

4. A description of /or location of the premises to be rented.

5. The starting and ending dates if it is a fixed-term tenancy.

6. The landlord's mailing address.

7. The amount of the security deposit, if any.

8. The name of the bank holding the security deposit.

9. Notice of the tenant's obligation to supply a forwarding address to the landlord within four days of terminating the tenancy.

10. Definition of responsibility for paying utilities.

11. Maintenance responsibilities.

12. Notice to quit procedures.

13. Any other agreements the landlord and tenant may wish to make.

My Former Addresses

Name: _____

Dates of Residency: _____ to _____

Address: _____

_____

Leased: _____ Owned: _____ Rented: _____

Name of Landlord: _____ Phone: _____

Address: _____

_____

Dates of Residency: _____ to _____

Address: _____

_____

Leased: _____ Owned: _____ Rented: _____

Name of Landlord: _____ Phone: _____

Address: _____

_____

Dates of Residency: _____ to _____

Address: _____

_____

Leased: _____ Owned: _____ Rented: _____

Name of Landlord: _____ Phone: _____

Address: _____

_____

Dates of Residency: _____ to _____

Address: _____

_____

Leased: _____ Owned: _____ Rented: _____

Name of Landlord: _____ Phone: _____

Address: _____

_____

How to Find a Roommate

When you share your home with another person, especially if you do not know them well, it can be a problem. It can help pay the bills and provide someone to talk with. However, if they do not pay their fair share of the bills, or use the place to entertain all their friends and this doesn't include you, it can be a problem.

Questions to ask a potential roommate:

1. Where they work and the hours they are at work.
2. What they like to do on weekends or holidays.
3. Are they in a relationship?
4. What are their rules for cleaning the house?
5. What are their rules for preparing food and cleaning up?
6. Do they need a phone and do they make long-distance calls?
7. What programs do they like on TV and how often do they watch TV?
8. What do they do with trash and do they recycle?
9. How long do they usually use the bathroom?
10. Do they have a car?
11. Are they safe with children?
12. Do they like animals?

When people live together in one home, there can be many boundary violations which lead to conflicts. What happens if the roommate does not help pay the rent? Will you be short of money to do it yourself? What if they leave a big mess? Who will clean it up if they refuse? What if their friends are not good around the kids?

If they have a criminal record, will you be included if something happens and the police are involved? Who will clean up, feed, and care for the animals? Who pays for damage done by the animals? Who pays for something that gets broken?

You need to check out the potential roommate and make sure that you will be compatible, or you will be ending up in a fight and no one is happy. You need to be sure the roommate will not harm your children or you can be involved in Child Protective services.

Remember: Don't assume… ASK!
Make sure your home is safe for you and your children.

Helpful Tips

1. Understand the Lease
    A lease, or rental agreement is a binding legal contract. You are liable for the rent payments as well as for anything else in the lease. Read the lease thoroughly!

    Unless the lease specifies that you are responsible for routine maintenance, such as shoveling snow, mowing the lawn, water bill, you have the right to expect the landlord to take care of these chores.

2. If you think you might be transferred or change jobs before your lease is up, try to negotiate a transfer clause. Short-term leases also can be arranged.

3. Find out what happens when the lease ends. Do you have to sign another lease or can you rent month-to-month?

4. Ask what is expected when you move out. Many landlords require a 30-day written notice.

5. Ask your landlord before you paint, wallpaper, carpet, or otherwise alter your space. Most landlords would rather you didn't make changes unless it is a real improvement. You could lose your security deposit or be evicted for breaking the rules.

6. If the place is a mess and you are handy, offer to fix it up. The landlord may deduct the cost of materials, and also for the labor, from your rent. Get any agreement in writing first!

7. One month's rent should be no more than one week of your gross income (that is before taxes). Look closely at your monthly expenses to make sure you don't get in over your head.

8. If you have roommates, make sure all names are on the lease. Try to get the landlord to accept separate agreements with each person, or get a written agreement between the roommates so you are liable only for your own share of the rent.

9. Know what you are renting. If a place has a basement, attic, or garage, and they are not listed for your use in the agreement, ask why. If you need or want to use them make sure the lease says you may.

10. Never sign anything or pay a deposit until you inspect the property and are absolutely sure you want to move in. If you change your mind after signing a lease and/or paying a deposit, you will lose your deposit and could even be sued.

Additional questions I may have: _____

_____

_____

_____

_____

Request for Rental Information Form

LANDLORD: Please complete all items below. Sign, date and include telephone number.

1. Name of renters): _____
   Number of people living in rental unit: _____
   Date renter moved into rental unit _____

2. Address of rental property: _
   City_____ Twp._____
   State _____ Zip Code _____

3. Type of rental unit:
   ☐ House ☐ Mobile Home ☐ Room
   ☐ Apartment ☐ Room and Bd ☐ Lot

4. Is the rental unit subsidized by:
   HUD ☐ yes ☐ no
   If yes, under what rental program(s) is it subsidized?
   Farmer's Home ☐ yes ☐ no

5. How often is rent due and how much does unit rent for?
   ☐ Monthly $_____
   ☐ Twice Monthly $_____
   ☐ Weekly $_____

   How much does the renter(s) listed in no. 1 pay?
   ☐ Monthly $_____
   ☐ Twice Monthly $_____
   ☐ Weekly $_____

   If room and board was checked in No. 3, what amount of the rent is for board (food)?
   ☐ Monthly $_____
   ☐ Twice Monthly $_____
   ☐ Weekly $_____

6. Is heating fuel included in the rent?
   ☐ yes ☐ no
   If no, which type of heating fuel is used to heat the unit?
   ☐ elec. ☐ Fuel Oil ☐ LP Gas (propane)
   ☐ Natural Gas ☐ Coal ☐ Other _____
   Does this unit's heat meter service more than one unit?
   ☐ yes ☐ no

7. Date this rental amount became effective:

   _____

8. Date last payment received?_____

9. Which of the following are included in the Rent?
   ☐ Electricity ☐ Gas/electric for ☐
   Hot water ☐ Garbage removal
   ☐ Water/sewage ☐ Other
   ☐ Gas/electric for stove/refrigerator

   Does this unit's electric meter service more than One unit? ☐ yes ☐ no

   APPLIANCES:
   ☐ Refrigerator ☐ Stove ☐ Washer ☐ Dryer

10. Name of property owner:_____
    Address: _____
    City:_____
    State: _____ Zip:_____
    Phone number:_____

11. Tax number or ID number of property owner:

    _____

12. Name of person to whom rent is paid if not property owner _____
    Address: _____
    City:_____
    State: _____ Zip:_____
    Phone number:_____

13. Is property owner related to anyone in rental unit?
    ☐ yes ☐ no

    If yes, to whom and relationship _____

    _____

14. Is person named in No. 12 related to anyone in rental unit?
    ☐ yes ☐ no

15. Are any property taxes for this rental unit overdue and unpaid?
    ☐ yes ☐ no

16. If vendor payments are made, who should payment notices be sent to? _____

17. Is rental unit in compliance with housing codes/ordinances?
    ☐ yes ☐ no

Signature of person completing this form:_____

Date:_____

Help with Housing

MSHDA—Michigan State Housing Development Authority

The State of Michigan has a program to help low-income families obtain housing. If you pay more than 30% of your family's income for rent and utilities, you may qualify for Federal Housing Assistance payments made on your behalf by the Michigan State Housing Development Authority directly to your landlord. First, you need to fill out an application to MSHDA. Then, you need to make an appointment for an interview. Look in the phone book for the phone number and address.

Finally, you will be put on a waiting list. If you qualify for the funding, you will be assured of money to help pay the rent. However, you need to find a place to rent yourself. Once you find housing and are receiving MSHDA assistance, you may not leave that home within a year, or you will lose the funding and have to reapply. If you reapply, you will be placed at the bottom of the waiting list again.

Here is a list of some documents that you will need to bring with you to the MSHDA interview:

- Copy of your lease with your name on it
- A pay stub
- Your driver's license
- State ID card
- Medicaid card
- Utility bill with your name on it
- Social security printout
- Voter's registration card or other proof of your residence or work address

Moving Checklist

Moving Tips: *3 to 4 weeks before move*
- [ ] Round up or purchase packing boxes
- [ ] Hold a garage sale for all items you will not be taking with you.
- [ ] Donate all items not sold at sale to charity. Get a signed receipt for your tax return.
- [ ] Inventory all items to be moved.
- [ ] Arrange for an estimate and method of payment from the moving company.
- [ ] Purchase full insurance coverage on all movables.
- [ ] Gather medical, dental records from doctors.
- [ ] Arrange for school to send transcripts to the new location.
- [ ] Check and clear tax assessments.
- [ ] Close local charge accounts.
- [ ] Arrange shipment of pet(s). Obtain pet immunization records from vet.
- [ ] Begin to use up food in freezer.
- [ ] Make hotel reservations, if necessary. Get a confirmation number.
- [ ] Fill out change-of-address cards with date of move. Turn into the post office.
- [ ] Send change-of-address cards to magazine companies.
- [ ] Keep a running list of all questions you may think of.

2 weeks before move:
- [ ] Clean and mend clothing items.
- [ ] Return all borrowed items and collect all things loaned out.
- [ ] Start packing.
- [ ] Transfer bank accounts.
- [ ] Arrange to disconnect/connect utilities.
- [ ] Service heavy appliances for move.
- [ ] Service car for trip.
- [ ] Arrange farewell parties, visits.

1 week before moving:
- [ ] Plan travel games, activities for children.
- [ ] Set aside and pack items to take in the car. Mark cartons, "DO NOT MOVE".
- [ ] Arrange for baby-sitter on moving day.
- [ ] Ask phone company if you can take the phones with you.
- [ ] Throw out all flammable items.
- [ ] Empty safe deposit box.
- [ ] Get pet tranquilizers if pet is to travel in car.

Day before moving:
- [ ] Empty, defrost and clean refrigerator and freezer. Let air for 24 hours.
- [ ] Clean stove and oven.
- [ ] Pack personal items.
- [ ] Ask police to place "No Parking" signs in front of your home if you live in an urban area. This will free a spot for the moving van.
- [ ] Take down drapes, rods, shelves, TV antenna.

Moving Day:
- [ ] Remain at home to answer questions.
- [ ] Vacuum and sweep home.
- [ ] Accompany moving personnel as your items are inventoried.
- [ ] Load vacuum last in van for fast cleanup in new home.
- [ ] Keep copies of all bills of lading. Be sure delivery address is correct.
- [ ] Confirm delivery date and time.
- [ ] Ask to be advised of final cost, which is calculated after the van is loaded and weighed.
- [ ] Be sure to have cash, money order or certified check to pay van operator before van is unloaded at destination.
- [ ] Check each room for forgotten items. Close and lock windows. Shut off lights.

Things I Need to Remember

A move is very stressful on everyone in the family, pets and children. Take time out to talk to your children about the move and let them help as much as they can. Try to make it a calm and enjoyable experience. After all, it is a new adventure and can be the best one yet!

Notes to myself:

_____

_____

_____

_____

_____

_____

_____

_____

_____

_____

_____

_____

_____

_____

_____

_____

_____

How to Choose a Pet

SECTION

11

Choosing and Caring for Pets

Having a living entity in your home means having responsibility for caring for it properly. A pet gives much love and loyalty, but needs much care also. If you cannot provide the kind of care that a pet needs, do not have one. You can always enjoy animals at the zoo, or volunteer at your local animal shelter, without the daily responsibility for them. However, if you decide that you want a pet to care for, here are some thoughts to help you make a good decision about what animal to get:

1. How much time and attention can you give your pet? Dogs and cats need interaction with their owners. Other pets, like ants, don't require more than a clean environment and food. If you work or go to school full-time, you may not have much time to spend with your pet.
   ☐ I can spend a lot of time. ☐ I don't have much time to spend.

2. How important is the cost to care for your pet to you? Some pets only need food and housing, other pets need frequent trips to the veterinarian. Animals, like snakes, need live food that also must be kept.
   ☐ I can spend the money on a pet. ☐ I don't have a lot of money to spend on a pet.

3. Do you want a larger or smaller pet?

4. How important is a quieter pet versus a noisy one?

5. How important is a smelly pet versus one with no odor?

6. Do you want a pet to have a certain look? ☐ I like soft fur. ☐ I like colorful feathers.
   ☐ I like smooth skin. ☐ I like a hard shell. ☐ I like scales.

7. How important is a pet with a longer life expectancy? Some pets live only a few months and others can live a long time, like 20 years.

8. What kind of house do you want to provide for your pet? Remember their house and bedding must be kept clean also. ☐ Cage ☐ Tank ☐ house ☐ stable

9. Do you want a pet that small children can handle also?

10. Is the pet you choose going to be legal in the neighborhood? Some pets must have special licenses or are prohibited in certain areas, like snakes and ferrets.

11. If you become ill and cannot care for your pet, who will take care of it for you? How will you see to your pet's care, if you decide you can't keep it?

Animal	Average Monthly Cost	Average Life Span
Dog	$35.00	11-15 years
Cat	$25.00	11 or more years
Gerbil	$5.00	5 years
Ferret	$15.00	6 to 10 years
Fish	$15.00	6 to 10 years
Frogs	$5.00	11 or more years
Mice/rats	$5.00	1 to 5 years
Birds	$25.00	11 or more years

Is Your Pet a Hazard to Your Health?

Many people are unaware that pets can carry diseases. Humans can contract rabies from a sick animal, although it is a rare occurrence. Besides allergies, cats can transmit a disease called toxoplasmosis to babies, that can be a potentially disabling infection that mothers contract during their pregnancy. Pregnant mothers are wise to avoid contact with the litter box. Have someone else change it. There are certain things a pet owner should know, whether the pet is a dog, cat, bird or lizard.

Roundworm and hookworm are common in both dogs and cats. About 99% of all puppies and kittens are born with roundworms, so pets should be treated by a veterinary doctor as soon as they are adopted. Children are particularly prone to parasite infection because they taste everything and are always putting their hands in their mouths. Be sure sandboxes are covered to avoid contamination and wash children's hands frequently if you have a pet.

Cats commonly spread ringworm and scabies, two skin afflictions. Cats also can carry a bacterium on their claws and in their mouths that is called "cat-scratch fever". Always clean any place your cat nips or scratches you and if you have an open wound, do not let the cat lick it.

While humans cannot catch feline leukemia, any cat that has this disease is very contagious to other cats and usually does not survive. Unfortunately, the virus stays in the house for a year following the death of the cat, so a new animal should not be brought into the home until well past a year.

Psittacosis is a respiratory disease that affects one-fourth of pet birds. It is transmitted to humans through droppings that dry out, and the dust can be inhaled. This disease can be treated, but if the symptoms persist for a long time, be sure to tell the doctor that you have a bird as a pet. To avoid this, keep the cage clean by changing the paper at the bottom of the cage every day. Wash the birdcage with hot soapy water once a week. When choosing a new bird, never pick one from a crowded cage.

Diseases from fish commonly come from cleaning a dirty tank and having a cut on a finger ,which causes an infection of the finger.

Reptiles can carry salmonella, which humans can get from contaminated food. Never keep a lizard or turtle in the kitchen and always wash hands after handling the pet or its tank.

If any member of your household is chronically ill or has a weakened immune system, you must be especially vigilant. Someone with AIDS, an elderly person, or a cancer patient undergoing chemotherapy will be at greater risk. As long as you take good care of your animals, you are taking good care of the entire family.

Wind Chill and Heat Index Tables

These tables list wind chills and heat indexes for various combinations of actual temperature and wind speed (or relative humidity). They are fairly self-explanatory, but here is a couple of examples: When it is 0∞ with a 10 m.p.h. wind, 20∞ with a 45 m.p.h. wind, or -22∞ with no wind, the wind chill is -22∞. Six months later, if it is 85∞ and the humidity reads 60%, the apparent temperature is 90∞ , but if the humidity is only 20%, the apparent temperature is 82∞. Asterisks (*) indicate combinations of temperature and humidity that are extremely unlikely (nothing's impossible though).

Wind Chill Index
Actual Temperature

Wind (MPH)	40	30	20	10	0	-10	-20	-30	-40	-50
0-4	40	30	20	10	0	-10	-20	-30	-40	-50
5	37	27	16	6	-5	-15	-26	-36	-47	-57
10	28	16	3	-9	-22	-34	-46	-58	-71	-83
15	23	9	-5	-18	-31	-45	-58	-72	-85	-99
20	19	4	-10	-24	-39	-53	-67	-81	-95	-110
25	16	1	-15	-29	-44	-59	-74	-88	-103	-117
30	13	-2	-18	-33	-49	-64	-79	-93	-109	-123
35	12	-4	-20	-35	-52	-67	-82	-97	-113	-128
40	11	-5	-21	-37	-53	-69	-84	-100	-115	-131
45	10	-6	-22	-38	-54	-70	-85	-102	-117	-133

Heat Index (Apparent Temperature)
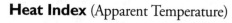
Actual Temperature vs. Relative Temperature

Humidity	70	75	80	85	90	95	100	105	110	115
0	64*	69*	73*	78*	83*	87*	91*	95*	99*	103*
10	65	70	75	80	85	90	95	100	105	111*
20	66	72	77	82	87	93	99	105	112	120*
30	67	73	78	84	90	96	104	113	123	135*
40	68	74	79	86	93	101	110	123	137*	151*
50	69	75	81	88	96	107	120	135*	150*	
60	70	76	83	90	100	114	132*	149*		
70	70	77	85	93	106	124*	144*			
80	71	78	87	97	113*	136*				
90	71	79	89	102*	122*					
100	72	80	91	108*						

Never leave your animals in an area that is too hot or too cold, whether inside or outside. Always be certain that they have fresh water to drink and shelter. Your children and your animals depend on you to provide for them so you must be fully aware of the conditions they are in at all times.

Record of Pet Immunizations

Pet's Name: _____ Date of Birth: _____

Immunizations:	Date:	Reactions:

Food Costs For My Pet

Brand of Food   Cost per pound: Total cost per week:

_____

_____

_____

_____

_____

_____

_____

_____

_____

Treats and toys

_____

_____

_____

_____

_____

Grooming Costs For My Pet

Date	Groomer	Was work satisfactory?	Cost

Medications and Vitamins For My Pet

Date	Medication	Treatment for	Results	Cost

Accidents and Illness of my Pet

Date	What happened	Treatment	Doctor	Cost

Consumer Knowledge

SECTION
12

Buying Guide

Every single item you buy will need to be cleaned, repaired and maintained through-out the time you own it. Some people are overwhelmed with "stuff"! This creates stress. So, it is very prudent to consider what "stuff" you must buy, need to buy, or want to buy. Impulse buying can be costly, more than just the purchase price. Before you purchase a large item or major product, sign a contract for home improvements, or seek professional help, take the time to research and consider the purchase. Here are some tips to think about:

1. **Compare the different brands.** Your friends or family may have their opinions about products they have used. There are consumer magazines and web sites with information also. Look for information on product comparisons.

2. **Compare vendors.** There can be a big difference on the cost and warranties offered on the same product. Even different pharmacies charge different prices for the same medications, so it pays to shop around.

3. **Look for customer satisfaction.** What attempts will the store make to have you satisfied?

4. **Ask about the store's return policy.**

5. **Read warranties before you buy a product.** Make sure you understand what you must do and what the manufacturer will do if you have a problem.

6. **Find out where repairs that come under the warranty take place.** Are repairs done at the store or sent out to another location? If it must be sent out, what happens if it is lost or damaged in transit? Is the repair shop reputable?

7. **Read the contract.** Make sure all the blank spaces are filled in or crossed out before you sign it.

8. **Be aware of extra costs.** All delivery fees and installation or other service charges should be spelled out before you buy. You may think the product is cheap, but the battery or bulb to make it work may be very expensive. Be sure you know how much it will cost in the future to keep it working also.

9. **Check with your state, county, and local agencies to find out if complaints have been lodged against the business.** The Better Business Bureau has information on retailers.

10. **To find home contractors, call your local housing authority to see if licensing and/or bonding are required.** If so, ask to see the contractor's license and bonding papers. Be sure that any contracting work done is free from any liens before making the final payment. (A lien can be made against the work if the contractor has not paid the person who did the work. If you pay the contractor and there are liens, you will have to pay the person yourself—paying twice for the same job. Not a good idea!)

11. Many licensing boards and professional and consumer associations offer referral services or educate consumers about what to look for.

Important Information to Keep

One of the most helpful skills is to keep information about the things you buy, especially major purchases. If you also pay for an extended warranty, record when it will expire and how much it will cost to maintain it. Remember that everything has a lifespan and the product may run out of useful life, so paying for extended warranty may not be cost effective. On the other hand, if repairs to the product will be costly, you may want to have the extra help for the costs by the extended warranty.

It helps to save the product information books, directions for assembly and parts lists, too.

Get a file box and place file folders with the following labels:

Large appliance information and warranties

refrigerator	water heater	pool equipment
stove	dishwasher	jacuzzi
furnace	air conditioner	more….

Small appliance information and warranties

radios	televisions	tape recorders
CD players	DVD players	fans
grooming tools	foot baths	

Workshop tools

saws	drills	tools
vises	lathes	shop vacs

Garden tools

rakes	shovels	blowers
mowers	tillers	snow blowers
chainsaws	branch trimmers	hedge trimmers

Kitchen tools

breadmakers	pasta makers	blenders
cuisenarts	microwaves	broilers
coffee makers	tea makers	espresso blenders

Electronics

computers	monitors	scanners
printers	sound accessories	cell phones

Toys

play stations	electronic toys	more…

Exercise and fitness equipment

bicycles	skateboards	surfboards
walkers	fitness equipment	heating pads
nebulizers	wheelchairs	massage equipment

Furniture information and warranties

mattresses	desks	chairs
bed	entertainment centers	
lawn furniture	more….	

Musical Instruments

| keyboards | guitars | instruments |
| pianos | organs | more… |

Art tools

| easel | sprayer | cutters |
| kilns | wheels | more…. |

Hobbies

| sewing machines | overlock machines |
| boat equipment | more….. |

Animals

| training equipment | grooming equipment |

As you can see, there are many areas that have important information that you may need. You may think of other areas that you need, but that have not been covered here. You might also like to keep the directions for assembly for future reference. You never know when you will need to replace a part or dismantle the object.

If you collect the information immediately upon bringing the item home and put it in the organized file, you will always be able to find it when you need it in case of repair or replacement. This information also helps for insurance purposes. Keep this file box in a safe place. You can maintain this file by putting the information with the item when you sell it at a yard sale, give it away or throw it out when the item is no longer working.

How to Complain

Oh dear! Something is not working right and you just bought it. You expected it to perform well. What do you do now? Knowing what to do, how and when to do it, is all part of the fine art of complaining. Successful complaining is an important skill. What works in one case may not work in another, but there is no doubt that you can save a lot of your time and energy by using these guidelines.

1. Act promptly. Pay attention at the cash register and go over bills and receipts before leaving a store or restaurant. Point out an error immediately and it is easily corrected.

2. Stay calm and collected. Blowing your top will waste your energy and block others from wanting to help you. This applies whether you are complaining in person, on the phone or by mail. You need cooperation, so start with this attitude. Just explain what went wrong.

3. Get information. When you think you have been "wronged," get information to help your case. Describe what you bought, give the date of purchase, the name of the person you dealt with, and the order or receipt number. If you want something repaired or replaced, get an estimate of the cost before lodging your complaint. Your state, county, city or town consumer protection agency will be able to tell you if a law has been broken, which law it is, and exactly what your rights are under the law. Write this information down and use it in all your phone calls and complaint letters. Those persons on the other end will know that you have done your homework and are serious about correcting the problem. Decide what you want and be specific on the action or remedy you are seeking.

4. Collect all copies of your records: sales slips, contracts and warranties. Never send the originals! You can also research your opponent—does this person or company have a history of doing this to customers? Does he resolve his complaints? The local Better Business Bureau may have answers to these questions.

5. Next, decide on how far you want to go. If you are getting the runaround with the company, find out what public or private agencies or organizations can help you. Who has the power to punish your opponent in some way—to take away his license or compel him to give your money back? Which groups are able and willing to mediate on your behalf? Better Business Bureaus, trade groups and many local and state consumer agencies offer some form of mediation. If all attempts at mediation have failed, you can contact a lawyer to attach his property and press on with a lawsuit. This will be expensive.

6. Keep records! Get into the habit of keeping all sales receipts. (You have a place to keep them with your money management plan. Organize and use the money management plan.) All warranties and contracts should be kept for as long as you have the product.

7. Once the complaint process begins, keep records of everything—names of people you have spoken to, dates, what they told you. If you do not get immediate satisfaction, you will need all this information in going to a higher authority.

8. The customer level—start with the salesperson or the customer service office. If you do not get results, go to the supervisor. If that fails, go to the store manager. Above that, write a letter to the company president, but be sure to get his name, address and phone number before you leave the store.

9. If you write a letter, explain what has happened, to what and when, indi-

cate which law has been broken (if true), and state exactly what you expect the company to do about it. Include the names of everyone you have spoken to and copies of your documentation. Tell the president of the company that you expect to have the matter resolved in 30 days.

10. At the highest level of complaining, in case you have not heard from the president of the company, it is time to escalate and to let the company know you have done so. Turn to those agencies you researched who can punish or mediate. Often letters addressed to the head of an agency by name get a higher level of attention than those addressed simply to Attorney General's Office or Office of Consumer Affairs.

11. Be persistent. Making consumer complaints can be frustrating and tiresome when you get no response. However, if you feel this is a complaint worth pursuing, keep at it. You can take the case to small claims court, but the monetary maximum is under $1,000.00. The good news is that, if you are organized, have your receipts and documentation, most complaints are resolved in a phone call or a letter or two. The complaints that are never resolved at all usually involve companies with a long history of abuse. The time you take to get information about the product before you buy it is time well spent and may save you the most money in the long run.

Purchase Contracts

Whenever you purchase a large item, such as appliances, furniture, property, or car, and you agree to pay a monthly fee to buy it, you must keep track of the payments carefully. Be certain to record the payments you make every time. You do not want to have to pay twice because you cannot prove you made the payment. Sometimes you can get a payment book, or you can make out a notebook of payments for yourself. This is a sample of a land contract form. Keep track of your rental payments also.

Date of Payment			Total Amount of Payment		Amount on Interest		Interest Paid to			Amount Paid on Principal		Balance of Principal		Signature (or initials)
Month	Day	Year					Month	Day	Year					

Comparing Loans

When you want to buy something, you should shop around for the best price. This is also true for financial institutions, such as banks, brokerages and loan institutions. Get at least three estimates and compare them. Then you can choose the one you wish to use.

Lender: _____   Lender: _____

Address: _____   Address: _____

_____   _____

Phone: _____   Phone: _____

Loan officer: _____   Loan officer: _____

Grace period: _____   Grace period: _____

Rebate for early loan repayment? _____   Rebate for early loan repayment? _____

Is there a discount for customers with _____   Is there a discount for customers with

other accounts? _____   other accounts? _____

Amount sought:$_____   Amount sought:$_____

To be: _____ secured loan   To be: _____ secured loan

_____ unsecured loan   _____ unsecured loan

12 Months

Annual Rate _____%   Annual Rate: _____%

Monthly payment:$_____   Monthly payment: $ _____

(x) 12   (=)$_____   (x) 12   (=) $ _____

Loan amount   (–)$_____   Loan amount   (–) $ _____

Total interest   (=) $ _____   Total interest   (=) $ _____

18 Months

Annual Rate _____%   Annual Rate: _____%

Monthly payment:$_____   Monthly payment: $ _____

(x) 12   (=)$_____   (x) 12   (=) $ _____

Loan amount   (–)$_____   Loan amount   (–) $ _____

Total interest   (=) $ _____   Total interest   (=) $ _____

24 Months

Annual Rate _____%   Annual Rate: _____%

Monthly payment:$_____   Monthly payment: $ _____

(x) 12   (=)$_____   (x) 12   (=) $ _____

Loan amount   (–)$_____   Loan amount   (–) $ _____

Total interest   (=) $ _____   Total interest   (=) $ _____

How to Buy a Used Car

Seller:_____ Phone:_____

Address: _____

Make and Model of car:_____ Year: _____

Vehicle ID #: _____

Mileage:_____ Is the care eligible for financing? _____

Warranty (if applicable):_____mi./ _____mos., at _____% parts and
_____% labor.

Evaluate the asking price (per used-car directory)   Base value: $ _____

Accessories: ☐ Air conditioning   ☐ Sunroof   ☐ vinyl roof
Sound system: ☐ Radio   ☐ Cassette   ☐ CD
Transmission: ☐ Automatic   ☐ Five speed
Windows: ☐ power
Other _____

Total accessories: $_____

(+) Base value: $_____

(=) Book value: $_____

(—) Needed repairs: $_____

(=) True value: $_____

Final price: $_____

State Sales Tax: $_____

(+) Registration fee: $_____

Total cost of used car: $_____

Inspection OK:

Check the following: headlights   parking lights   brake lights   turn signals
                        emergency flasher   interior lights   instrument panel   windshield wipers
                        spare tire and jack visible body damage

During the test drive, check the following OK:
            heater   power windows   radio/cassette   air conditioning
            muffler   acceleration   braking   steering
            suspension   overall handling unusual noises

An independent mechanic can inspect the car for a fee and tell you what would need to be repaired and how much it would cost.

Car Mileage Log and Maintenance Record

Obtain a small ledger book and write the following log. Keep it in the car and write down the information every time the car is serviced, you get gas or other information.

Date	Mileage	Maintenance	Gal. Of fuel	Cost of fuel		Miles per gallon

Car Mileage Log and Maintenance Record

Obtain a small ledger book and write the following log. Keep it in the car and write down the information every time the car is serviced, you get gas or other information.

Date	Mileage	Maintenance	Gal. Of fuel	Cost of fuel		Miles per gallon

Keep in glove compartment or in car log book

Make: _____

Model: _____

Year: _____

Color: _____ Weight: _____

Vehicle ID#: _____

Owner: _____

Address: _____

Dealer: _____ Phone: _____

License Plate #: _____ State: _____ Expires: _____ / _____

Warranty expires: _____ / _____

Emergency road service: _____ ID# _____

Garage: _____ Address: _____ Phone: _____

Doctor: _____ Address: _____ Phone: _____

Attorney: _____ Address: _____ Phone: _____

Insurance Company: _____ Agent: _____

Address: _____ Phone: _____

Checklist for on-the-road breakdowns:

blanket	flares/reflectors	pencil and paper	tools: hammer, pliers,
change	flashlight	snow/ice scraper	screwdrivers, wrench
electrical tape	jumper cables	spare tire, jack and tire iron	
fire extinguisher	first-aid kit	paper toweling	work gloves

In a Medical Emergency (list the people who are frequent passengers in this car)

Name: _____ Birth date: _____ Sex: _____ Blood type: _____

Height: _____ Weight: _____ Hair: _____ Eyes: _____

Address: _____ Phone: _____

Name: _____ Birth date: _____ Sex: _____ Blood type: _____

Height: _____ Weight: _____ Hair: _____ Eyes: _____

Address: _____ Phone: _____

Driver's License #: _____ State: _____

In an emergency, call: _____

Organ Donor: ☐ no ☐ yes Notify: _____ Phone: _____

Negative and Positive Methods of Communication

The power that we have is located in the manner in which we speak with other people. It is difficult to have perfect communication, but good communication is a learned skill, and the more we practice it, the better we get. Many times, in our talking with others, we say more than we intend or say things we really do not mean to say. How we say it is also communication and gives different messages. Our body language imparts a great deal of information in a silent manner. Here are some communication manners that we need to be aware of:

1. Warning, admonishing, threatening—telling someone that consequences will occur if they do or do not do something.

2. Exhorting, preaching, moralizing—telling someone what they ought to do (in your opinion).

3. Ordering, commanding, directing—a person to do something.

4. Advising, giving solutions or suggestions—telling someone how to solve a problem, giving advice or suggestions.

5. Lecturing, teaching, giving logical arguments—trying to influence someone with facts, counter-arguments, logic, information or other opinions.

6. Judging, criticizing, disagreeing, blaming—making a negative judgment or evaluation of the person.

7. Name-calling, ridiculing, shaming—making a person feel foolish, labeling.

8. Analyzing, interpreting, diagnosing—telling someone what their motives are or analyzing why they are doing or saying something.

While we need to be careful in our negotiation with others when we are building a cooperative effort, we also need to be careful in our communication with our closest family and friends. It is easy to forget that they have feelings too. Our children hear what we tell them and believe that what we say is true. If we speak in a positive manner, our children will thrive and succeed. Both positive and negative communication always leaves an impression!

How is Your Life Balance?

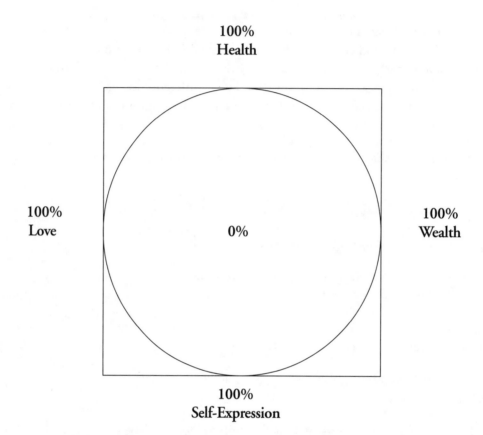

100%
Health

100%   0%   100%
Love   Wealth

100%
Self-Expression

Each value is from 0% to 100%. Choose a value that you think indicates this factor in your life's balance. Then connect the dots.

A balanced life should show a full circle. If you do not have a full circle, what areas should you take a serious look at to help you lead a more fully balanced life?

Evaluation Form

Just as this guidebook has been about taking an honest look at where you are in your life, we too, need to examine what works and what doesn't. Please respond to the following questions and let us know what you think needs to be added, taken out or changed in this book.

1. This guidebook was most helpful by _____
    _____
    _____

2. I did not find the following areas helpful to me _____
    _____
    _____

3. I would like to see more information added in _____
    _____

4. I would like to see the following changes made _____
    _____
    _____

5. I found some typos on pages _____

6. I would recommend this guidebook to my friends ☐ yes ☐ no

7. I have found a mentor to help me discuss areas in this guidebook and make the changes I need to make in my life to be more successful. ☐ yes ☐ no

8. Other comments I want to make _____

Thank you for your contribution in your comments. We want to improve our service to you and will make recommended changes in the next edition that will make this guidebook more useful.

Mail this completed page to:

Leni Cowling, MEd, LPC, HRD
P.O. Box 892
Bellaire, MI 49615

Order form

To order a copy of Successful Living Skills: The Puzzle of Families

Send $49.95 per copy
Plus .06% MI sales tax

To

Successful Living Skills: The Puzzle of Families
Family-information
Leni Cowling
P.O. Box 892
Bellaire, MI 49615